Robert Rose's
Favorite
PASTA

Robert
ROSE

ROBERT ROSE'S FAVORITE PASTA

Canadian Cataloguing in Publication Data

Main entry under title:

Robert Rose's favorite pasta

Includes index.

ISBN 1-896503-74-8

1. Cookery (Pasta).   I. Title: Classic pasta.

TX809.M17R63 1998   641.8'22   C97-932609-5

DESIGN AND PAGE COMPOSITION: MATTHEWS COMMUNICATIONS DESIGN
PHOTOGRAPHY: MARK T. SHAPIRO, RICHARD ALLEN

Cover photo: (PENNE WITH STEAK, PLUM TOMATOES AND PESTO, PAGE 61)

Distributed in the U.S. by:
Firefly Books (U.S.) Inc.
P.O. Box 1338
Ellicott Station
Buffalo, NY   14205

Distributed in Canada by:
Stoddart Publishing Co. Ltd.
34 Lesmill Road
North York, Ontario
M3B 2T6

ORDER LINES
Tel: (416) 499-8412
Fax: (416) 499-8313

ORDER LINES
Tel: (416) 445-3333
Fax: (416) 445-5967

Published by: Robert Rose Inc. • 156 Duncan Mill Road, Suite 12
Toronto, Ontario, Canada M3B 2N2   Tel: (416) 449-3535

Printed in Canada   234567 BP 01 00 99 98

About this book

At Robert Rose, we're committed to finding imaginative and exciting ways to provide our readers with cookbooks that offer great recipes — and exceptional value. That's the thinking behind our new "Robert Rose's Favorite" series.

Here we've selected over 50 favorite pasta recipes from a number of our bestselling full-sized cookbooks: Byron Ayanoglu's *New Vegetarian Gourmet*; Johanna Burkhard's *Comfort Food Cookbook*; Andrew Chase's *Asian Bistro Cookbook*; *New Wordle Noodles*, by Bill Jones and Stephen Wong; and Rose Reisman's *Light Cooking, Light Pasta* and *Enlightened Home Cooking*. As well, we've included recipes from our own *Robert Rose's Classic Pasta*.

We believe that it all adds up to great value for any pasta lover.

Want to find out more about the sources of our recipes? See page 96 for details.

Contents

Chicken

Meat

Vegetables

Stuffed & Baked Pasta

Soups

Serves 6

Chicken Pasta Vegetable Bean Minestrone

2 tsp	vegetable oil	10 mL
1 tsp	crushed garlic	5 mL
3/4 cup	chopped onions	175 mL
3/4 cup	finely chopped carrots	175 mL
1 cup	sliced mushrooms	250 mL
1 cup	diced sweet potatoes	250 mL
5 cups	chicken stock	1.25 L
1 cup	canned red kidney beans or chick peas, drained	250 mL
6 oz	skinless boneless chicken breast, diced	150 g
1 cup	chopped broccoli	250 mL
1/3 cup	small shell pasta *or* broken linguine	75 mL
1/4 cup	chopped parsley	50 mL

1. In a large nonstick saucepan, heat oil; sauté garlic, onions and carrots until tender, approximately 7 minutes. Add mushrooms and sauté for 4 minutes.

2. Add sweet potatoes, stock and beans. Cover and simmer over low heat for 12 minutes or until sweet potatoes are just tender.

3. Add chicken, broccoli and pasta; simmer for 7 minutes or until pasta and chicken are cooked. Sprinkle with parsley.

Tomato Vegetable Pasta Soup

Serves 6

TIP

A medium onion can replace leek.

•

Sweet potatoes can replace regular potatoes to give a unique sweetness to this soup.

•

Any small shell pasta can be used.

MAKE AHEAD

Prepare soup early in day. Do not add pasta until 10 minutes before serving.

FROM
ROSE REISMAN
BRINGS HOME LIGHT PASTA

2 tsp	vegetable oil	10 mL
1 1/2 tsp	crushed garlic	7 mL
1	medium leek, sliced	1
1 cup	thinly sliced carrots	250 mL
1 cup	sliced celery	250 mL
1 cup	diced potatoes	250 mL
4 cups	chicken broth	1 L
1	can (19 oz [540 mL]) crushed tomatoes	1
1 1/2 cups	canned white kidney beans, drained	375 mL
1	bay leaf	1
1 1/2 tsp	dried basil	7 mL
1 tsp	dried oregano	5 mL
1/3 cup	broken linguine	75 mL

1. In a large nonstick saucepan sprayed with vegetable spray, heat oil; sauté garlic, leek, carrots and celery until tender.

2. Add potatoes, broth, tomatoes, beans, bay leaf, basil and oregano. Cover and simmer on medium heat for 20 minutes or until potatoes are tender.

3. Add pasta and cook for 10 minutes or until pasta is cooked.

Chunky Veal Stew over Rigatoni

12 oz	rigatoni	375 g
2 tsp	vegetable oil	10 mL
12 oz	boneless stewing veal, cut into 1-inch (2.5 cm) cubes	375 g
2 tsp	crushed garlic	10 mL
1 cup	chopped onions	250 mL
3/4 cup	diced carrots	175 mL
1 cup	sliced zucchini	250 mL
1/3 cup	dry red wine	75 mL
1 cup	sliced mushrooms	250 mL
1 cup	beef or chicken stock	250 mL
1	can (19 oz [540 mL]) crushed tomatoes	1
2 tbsp	tomato paste	25 mL
1	bay leaf	1
2 tsp	chili powder	10 mL
2 tsp	dried basil	10 mL
1 1/2 tsp	dried oregano	7 mL
1/3 cup	grated Parmesan cheese	75 mL
	Pepper	

1. Cook pasta in boiling water according to package instructions or until firm to the bite. Drain and place in serving bowl.

2. In a medium nonstick saucepan sprayed with vegetable spray, add 1 tsp (5 mL) oil. Sauté veal until browned on all sides, approximately 4 minutes. Remove meat and set aside.

3. Add the remaining 1 tsp (5 mL) oil to saucepan and sauté garlic, onions, carrots and zucchini until tender, approximately 5 minutes. Add wine and cook for 2 minutes. Add mushrooms and sauté for 4 minutes. Add stock, tomatoes and tomato paste, bay leaf, chili powder, basil, oregano and veal. Cover and simmer for 50 to 60 minutes or until veal is tender. Pour over pasta. Sprinkle with cheese and pepper, and toss.

Serves 4

**as a main course or 6
as a starter**

Shredded Chicken, Mushroom and Egg Noodle Soup

TIP

Chicken soup is known as a great comfort food and this recipe — which produces a nourishing and satisfying meal — lives up to that standard.

•

You can use leftover chicken, but for the best results use a good stock.

**FROM
NEW WORLD NOODLES
BY BILL JONES & STEPHEN WONG**

1 tbsp	vegetable oil	15 mL
1	onion, thinly sliced	1
1 tbsp	minced garlic	15 mL
1 cup	sliced mushrooms	250 mL
1	carrot, peeled and grated	1
1 tbsp	hoisin sauce	15 mL
1 cup	shredded cooked chicken	250 mL
6 cups	chicken stock	1.5 L
1 cup	thin dried egg noodles, crushed	250 mL
1 tsp	sesame oil	5 mL
1	green onion, sliced	1
	Salt and pepper to taste	

1. In a large saucepan, heat oil over medium-high heat for 30 seconds. Add onion and cook until it softens and begins to change color. Add garlic, mushrooms and carrot; sauté for 1 minute. Add hoisin sauce, chicken, stock and noodles; stir until well mixed.

2. Bring mixture to a boil; reduce heat and simmer for 5 minutes or until the noodles are soft. Season with salt and pepper to taste. Drizzle with sesame oil and garnish with green onion. Serve immediately.

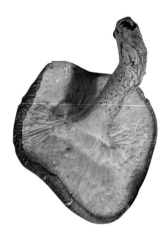

Salads

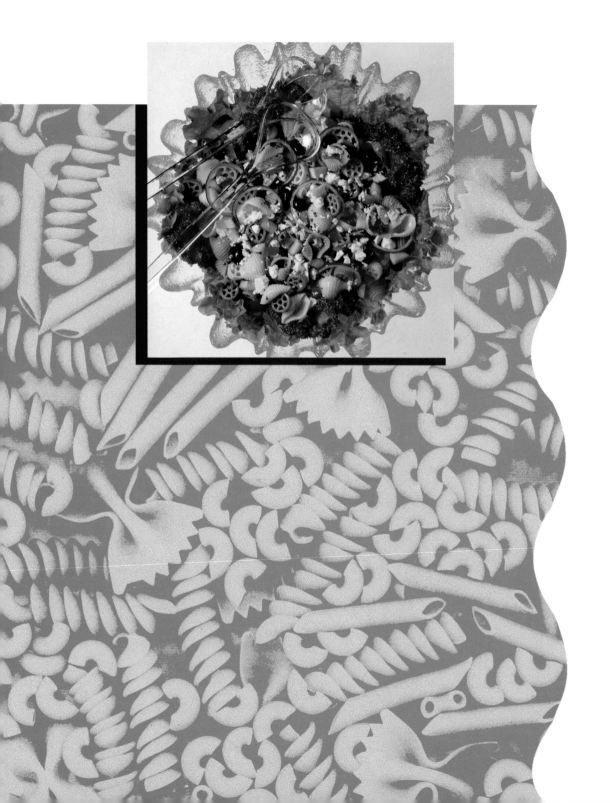

Serves 6

as an appetizer.

Mango Salsa over Vermicelli

TIP

Use a ripe sweet mango for a more intense flavor. If unripe, mangoes are unpleasantly sour.

MAKE AHEAD

Prepare salsa early in day and refrigerate. (This will also allow it to develop more flavor.) Pour over pasta just before serving.

FROM
ROSE REISMAN BRINGS HOME LIGHT PASTA

8 oz	vermicelli or other fine-strand pasta	250 g
1 3/4 cups	diced mangoes	425 mL
3/4 cup	diced red bell peppers	175 mL
1/2 cup	diced red onions	125 mL
1/2 cup	diced green peppers	125 mL
3 tbsp	olive oil	45 mL
3 tbsp	lemon juice	45 mL
2 tsp	crushed garlic	10 mL
1/2 cup	chopped coriander or parsley	125 mL

1. Cook pasta in boiling water according to package instructions or until firm to the bite. Rinse with cold water. Drain and set aside.

2. In bowl of food processor, combine mangoes, red peppers, onions, green peppers, oil, lemon juice, garlic and coriander. Process on and off just until finely diced. Pour over pasta; serve at room temperature.

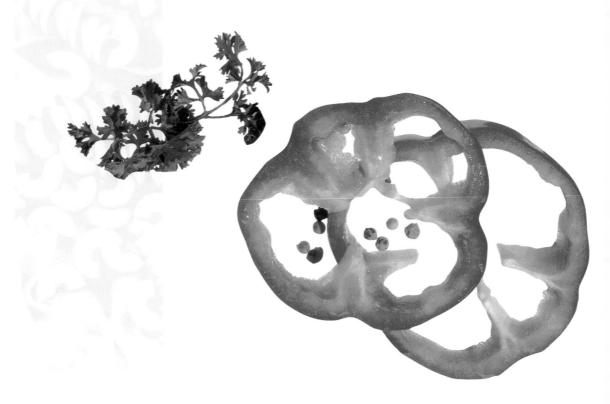

Rotini Niçoise

12 oz	rotini	375 g
6 oz	green beans, cut in pieces	150 g
1 3/4 cups	chopped tomatoes	425 mL
3/4 cup	diced cucumbers	175 mL
3/4 cup	diced sweet red or green peppers	175 mL
1/2 cup	sliced red onions	125 mL
1	can (6.5 oz [185g]) flaked tuna packed in water, drained	1
1/3 cup	sliced olives	75 mL
1/2 cup	chopped fresh dill (or 1 tbsp [15 mL] dried)	125 mL
5	anchovies, minced	5

Dressing

1/3 cup	olive oil	75 mL
1/4 cup	lemon juice	50 mL
1/4 cup	balsamic vinegar	50 mL
2 tbsp	water	25 mL
2 tsp	crushed garlic	10 mL
	Cucumber shavings	

1. Cook pasta in boiling water according to package instructions or until firm to the bite. Rinse with cold water. Drain and place in serving bowl.

2. Blanch green beans in boiling water just until still crisp, approximately 2 minutes. Drain, rinse with cold water and add to pasta. Add tomatoes, cucumbers, sweet peppers, onions, tuna, olives, dill and anchovies.

3. Make the dressing: In a small bowl combine oil, lemon juice, vinegar, water and garlic. Pour over pasta, and toss. Garnish with cucumber shavings.

Warm Caesar Pasta Salad

Sauce

1	egg	1
3	anchovies, chopped	3
3 tbsp	olive oil	45 mL
2 tbsp	grated Parmesan cheese	25 mL
1 tbsp	lemon juice	15 mL
1 tbsp	red wine vinegar	15 mL
2 tsp	Dijon mustard	10 mL
1 1/2 tsp	minced garlic	7 mL
2 cups	washed, dried and torn romaine lettuce	500 mL
2 oz	prosciutto, shredded	50 g
12 oz	penne	375 g

1. Put egg, anchovies, olive oil, Parmesan, lemon juice, vinegar, mustard and garlic in food processor; process until smooth.

2. Put lettuce and prosciutto in large serving bowl. In large pot of boiling water, cook pasta according to package directions or until tender but firm; drain and add to serving bowl. Pour dressing over pasta and toss.

Corn and Three-Bean Salad

8 oz	pasta wheels or small shell pasta	250 g
1 cup	canned black beans or chick peas, drained	250 mL
3/4 cup	canned red kidney beans, drained	175 mL
3/4 cup	canned white kidney beans, drained	175 mL
3/4 cup	canned corn niblets, drained	175 mL
1 1/4 cups	diced sweet red peppers	300 mL
3/4 cup	diced carrots	175 mL
1/2 cup	diced red onions	125 mL

FROM
ROSE REISMAN BRINGS HOME
LIGHT PASTA

Dressing

1/4 cup	lemon juice	50 mL
3 tbsp	vegetable oil	45 mL
3 tbsp	red wine or cider vinegar	45 mL
2 tsp	crushed garlic	10 mL
1/2 cup	chopped coriander or parsley	125 mL

1. Cook pasta in boiling water according to package instructions or until firm to the bite. Rinse with cold water. Drain and place in serving bowl.

2. Add all three beans, corn niblets, red peppers, carrots and onions.

3. Make the dressing: In small bowl combine lemon juice, oil, vinegar, garlic and coriander. Pour over dressing, and toss.

Serves 4 to 6

Pasta Salad with Black Olives and Feta Cheese

TIP

Substitute one small regular field cucumber if pickling cucumbers are unavailable.

— *City Restaurant* —
LOS ANGELES

FROM
THE ROBERT ROSE BOOK OF
CLASSIC PASTA

12 oz	small shell pasta	375 g
3/4 cup	olive oil	175 mL
8 oz	feta cheese, crumbled	250 g
3/4 cup	sliced black olives	175 mL
3	kirby or pickling cucumbers, diced	3
2	tomatoes, diced	2
1	red onion, thinly sliced	1
1/4 cup	chopped fresh oregano (or 4 tsp [20 mL] dried)	50 mL
Dash	hot pepper sauce (optional)	Dash
	Salt and pepper to taste	

1. In a large pot of boiling salted water, cook small shell pasta 8 to 10 minutes or until *al dente*; drain. Rinse under cold water and drain. Toss with 1/4 cup (50 mL) of the olive oil.

2. In a bowl stir together remaining olive oil, feta cheese, olives, cucumbers, tomatoes, red onion, oregano and hot pepper sauce, if desired.

3. Toss pasta with dressing; season to taste with salt and pepper. Chill before serving.

Pasta salads are always a hit. They brighten up a buffet, backyard barbecue or your dinner table. Served with Herbed Garlic Bread this salad is a meal in itself.

TIP

You can also add 8 oz (125 g) pepperoni, salami or ham, cut into thin 1-inch (2.5 cm) strips.

•

Dried basil and oregano can be replaced with 1 tbsp (15 mL) each chopped fresh. (As a general rule, when substituting fresh for dried herbs use 3 times the amount of fresh for the dried.)

FROM
THE COMFORT FOOD COOKBOOK
BY JOANNA BURKHARD

Italian Pasta Salad

Salad

8 oz	pasta such as fusilli or penne	250 g
4 oz	Provolone cheese, cut into small cubes	125 g
1 cup	cherry tomatoes, halved or quartered, if large	250 mL
1/3 cup	diced red onions	75 mL
Half	large sweet red pepper, cut into thin 1 1/2-inch (4 cm) strips	Half
Half	large sweet green pepper, cut into thin 1 1/2-inch (4 cm) strips	Half
1/3 cup	Kalamata olives (optional)	75 mL
1/3 cup	finely chopped fresh parsley	75 mL

Dressing

1/4 cup	olive oil	50 mL
2 tbsp	red wine vinegar	25 mL
1 tbsp	Dijon mustard	15 mL
1	large clove garlic, minced	1
1 tsp	dried basil	5 mL
1 tsp	dried oregano	5 mL
1/2 tsp	salt	2 mL
1/4 tsp	pepper	1 mL

1. Cook pasta in a large pot of boiling salted water until tender but still firm. Drain; rinse under cold water and drain well.

2. In a large serving bowl, combine pasta, cheese cubes, tomatoes, onions, peppers, olives and parsley.

3. In a bowl combine oil, vinegar, mustard, garlic, basil, oregano, salt and pepper.

4. Pour dressing over pasta mixture; toss until well-coated. Let stand at room temperature for up to 30 minutes, allowing flavors to blend. Refrigerate if making ahead.

Broad Egg Noodle and Vegetable Salad with a Spicy Black Bean Vinaigrette

Serves 4

TIP

If you're too impatient to whisk this robust vinaigrette by hand, use a blender. Just add the oil in a steady stream.

•

The dressing also works well with any green salad. But make sure you add green vegetables just before serving — otherwise they'll turn a drab and unappealing shade of green.

FROM
NEW WORLD NOODLES
BY BILL JONES & STEPHEN WONG

Vinaigrette

1 tbsp	dark soya sauce	15 mL
1/2 cup	rice vinegar	125 mL
2 tbsp	black bean sauce	25 mL
2 tbsp	honey	25 mL
1 tbsp	prepared mustard, such as Dijon	15 mL
1 tsp	chili paste	5 tsp
2 tbsp	water	25 mL
1 cup	vegetable oil	250 mL

Salad

1 lb	fresh broad egg noodles *or* 8 oz (250 g) dried fettuccine or linguine	500 g
1 tbsp	vegetable oil	15 mL
1	carrot, peeled and thinly sliced	1
1 tbsp	minced ginger root	15 mL
1 tbsp	minced garlic	15 mL
2 cups	thinly sliced Chinese broccoli *or* broccoli	500 mL
2 cups	shredded Chinese cabbage *or* green cabbage	500 mL
2	whole green onions, thinly sliced	2

1. In a large bowl, combine soya sauce, vinegar, black bean sauce, honey, mustard, chili paste and water; add oil in a steady stream, whisking constantly to emulsify. Set aside.

2. If using fresh noodles, cut into 4-inch (10 cm) strips. (If using dried pasta, break strands in half.)

3. In a large pot of boiling salted water, cook noodles until *al dente*, about 4 to 5 minutes. (If using pasta, prepare according to package directions.) Drain, coat with a little oil and set aside.

4. In a nonstick wok or skillet, heat oil over high for 30 seconds. Add carrots, ginger root and garlic. Sauté for 2 to 3 minutes. Add broccoli and cook until tender, about 2 minutes. Season with salt and pepper and remove from heat.

5. In a large bowl, combine vinaigrette, noodles, vegetable mixture and Chinese cabbage; toss. Garnish with green onions and serve immediately.

Serves 4

Rice Noodle Salad with Sugar Snap Peas, Sweet Peppers and Almonds with Nuoc Cham

TIP

To toast almonds, heat a dry heavy skillet over medium heat for 30 seconds. Add almonds and cook until they begin to turn golden, about 2 minutes. Immediately remove from heat, as they'll continue cooking until they cool.

FROM
NEW WORLD NOODLES
BY BILL JONES & STEPHEN WONG

8 oz	medium vermicelli (rice stick noodles) *or* dried fettuccine	250 g
2/3 cup	*nuoc cham* (Vietnamese dipping sauce)	150 mL
1 tbsp	butter	15 mL
1 tbsp	olive oil	15 mL
3 cups	trimmed sugar snap or snow peas	750 mL
2 tsp	minced garlic	10 mL
2 tbsp	vegetable or chicken stock	25 mL
1 cup	thinly sliced red bell peppers	250 mL
1 cup	thinly sliced yellow bell peppers	250 mL
1/2 cup	toasted sliced almonds	125 mL
1/4 cup	cilantro (fresh coriander) leaves	50 mL
	Coarsely ground black pepper, to taste	

1. In a heatproof bowl or pot, cover noodles with boiling water and soak for 5 minutes. (If using pasta, prepare according to package directions.) Drain, toss with 1/3 cup (75 mL) of the *nuoc cham* and let cool to room temperature.

2. In a nonstick pan, heat butter and oil over medium-high heat until just smoking. Add peas and stir-fry until well-coated, about 30 seconds. Add garlic and stock. Cover and cook until peas are tender-crisp, about 1 minute. Add peppers and stir-fry until warmed through and liquid is absorbed, about 1 minute. Remove from heat. Add remaining *nuoc cham* and mix well.

3. In a large salad bowl, combine noodles, vegetables, almonds and cilantro; toss. Sprinkle with black pepper to taste and serve.

Pasta & Sauce

FROM
THE NEW VEGETARIAN GOURMET
BYRON AYANOGLU

Linguine Barolo

1/2 lb	linguine	250 g
2 tbsp	olive oil	25 mL
3/4 cup	10% cream	175 mL
	or	
	double-strength vegetable stock (1 1/2 cups [375 mL] reduced to half) bolstered with 2 tbsp (25 mL) olive oil	
2 oz	Gorgonzola cheese, crumbled	50 g
4	sun-dried tomatoes, cut into 1/2-inch (1 cm) strips	4
1 1/2 cups	broccoli florets	375 mL
1/4 cup	toasted pine nuts	50 mL
	Few sprigs fresh parsley, chopped	

1. In a large pot of boiling salted water, cook pasta according to package directions until tender but firm. Drain pasta and add olive oil; toss until well coated. Cover and set aside.

2. In a skillet heat the cream (or oiled broth, if using) over medium heat until it begins to steam. Add Gorgonzola and stir until cheese has dissolved (about 2 minutes). Reduce heat to medium-low and add sun-dried tomatoes and broccoli; continue cooking, stirring occasionally, until the sauce is smooth and the broccoli tender, about 4 to 5 minutes.

3. Add the linguine and raise heat back to medium. Toss and cook for 2 to 3 minutes, until pasta is well coated and heated through. Serve garnished with pine nuts and parsley.

Serves 4

TIP

Other pastas such as rotini or even fettuccine will suit this spicy tomato sauce.

•

For a spicier sauce, increase the capers and red pepper flakes.

MAKE AHEAD

Sauce can be prepared and refrigerated 2 days in advance, or frozen up to 1 month.

FROM
ROSE REISMAN BRINGS HOME
LIGHT COOKING

Penne with Spicy Marinara Sauce

1 1/2 tsp	vegetable oil	7 mL
1/2 cup	chopped onions	125 mL
1 tsp	crushed garlic	5 mL
1 1/2 tsp	capers	7 mL
1	can (19 oz [540 mL]) tomatoes, puréed	1
1/3 cup	sliced pitted black olives	75 mL
1 tbsp	tomato paste	15 mL
1 1/2 tsp	dried basil (or 3 tbsp [45 mL] chopped fresh)	7 mL
1/2 tsp	dried oregano	2 mL
1	bay leaf	1
	Red pepper flakes	
8 oz	penne	250 g
4 tsp	grated Parmesan cheese	20 mL

1. In large nonstick skillet, heat oil; sauté onions, garlic and capers for 3 minutes.

2. Add tomatoes, olives, tomato paste, basil, oregano, bay leaf, and red pepper flakes to taste; cover and simmer for 10 to 15 minutes or until thickened slightly and flavors are blended. Discard bay leaf.

3. Meanwhile, cook penne according to package directions or until firm to the bite. Drain and place in serving bowl. Toss with sauce. Sprinkle with cheese.

Serves 4 to 6

Rigatoni with Roasted Ratatouille Sauce

PREHEAT OVEN TO 400° F (200° C)
12- BY 8-INCH (2.5 L) SHALLOW BAKING DISH

1	eggplant (about 1 lb [500 g])	1
2	medium zucchini (about 12 oz [375 g])	2
1	large sweet red pepper	1

Chockfull of vegetables, this zesty tomato sauce can be used in a variety of ways.I use it as a pizza sauce, as a topping for creamy polenta, or to dress baked potatoes. Instead of sautéeing the vegetables in batches on the stovetop, I've stream-lined the method by roast-ing them in the oven.

TIP

Red pepper flakes are sold with a variety of names, including crushed dried chilies or hot chili pepper flakes. You can find them in supermarkets and in bulk foods shops. Other sources of hot seasonings such as cayenne pepper can be substituted, but use slightly less (it's hotter).

FROM
THE COMFORT FOOD COOKBOOK
BY JOANNA BURKHARD

2 tbsp	olive oil	25 mL
	Salt and pepper	
1	large onion, finely chopped	1
2	large cloves garlic, minced	2
1 tsp	dried basil	5 mL
1 tsp	dried oregano	5 mL
1/4 tsp	dried thyme	1 mL
1/4 tsp	red pepper flakes, or to taste	1 mL
1	can (28 oz [796 mL]) plum tomatoes, juice reserved, chopped	1
1/4 cup	chopped fresh parsley	50 mL
8 oz	rigatoni *or* other tube-shaped pasta	250 g
1 1/2 cups	shredded mozzarella *or* Provolone cheese	375 mL

1. Cut eggplant, zucchini and peppers into 3/4-inch (2 cm) cubes. Arrange vegetables on oiled rimmed baking sheet. Toss with 1 tbsp (15 mL) of the oil; season with salt and pepper.

2. Roast, uncovered, in preheated oven, stirring occasionally, for 35 minutes or until vegetables are tender and lightly colored.

3. Meanwhile, in a large saucepan, heat remaining oil over medium heat. Add onion, garlic, basil, oregano, salt, sugar, thyme and red pepper flakes; cook, stirring often, for 4 minutes or until softened.

4. Add tomatoes with juice; bring to a boil, reduce heat to medium-low and simmer, partially covered, for 20 minutes.

5. Add roasted vegetables and parsley; simmer for 5 minutes to blend flavors. Adjust seasoning with salt and pepper to taste.

6. Cook pasta in a large pot of boiling salted water until tender but firm. Drain well. Toss with vegetable sauce; spoon into baking dish. Sprinkle with cheese.

7. Bake in preheated oven for 25 to 30 minutes (10 minutes longer if refrigerated) or until bubbly and cheese is lightly colored.

Serves 4 to 6

As popular today as in the 1950s, classic macaroni and cheese has a lot going for it. It's not hard to make, so why open up a box of the pre-packaged stuff when you can create the real thing in your kitchen?

TIPS

You can ruin a good pasta dish if you don't cook the pasta properly. The most common error is not using enough water to boil the pasta — with the result that it cooks unevenly and sticks together.

•

How to cook 1 lb (500 g) of pasta: Using a large pot, bring 16 cups (4 L) of water to a full rolling boil. Add 1 tbsp (15 mL) salt (this is important for flavor) and all the pasta at once. (Do not add oil.) Stir immediately to prevent pasta from sticking. Cover with a lid to return water quickly to full boil. Then uncover and stir occasionally. Taste to see if pasta is al dente, or firm to the bite. Drain immediately. Unless directed otherwise, never rinse pasta — this chills it and removes the coating of starch that helps sauce cling to pasta. Return to pot or place in large warmed serving bowl; add the sauce and toss until well-coated. (Never plunk pasta on serving plates and ladle sauce on top.) Serve immediately.

FROM
THE COMFORT FOOD COOKBOOK
BY JOANNA BURKHARD

Best-Ever Macaroni and Cheese

PREHEAT OVEN TO 375° F (190° C)
8-CUP (2 L) DEEP CASSEROLE DISH, BUTTERED

Cheese Sauce

3 tbsp	butter	45 mL
1/4 cup	all-purpose flour	50 mL
1	bay leaf	1
3 cups	milk	750 mL
1 tbsp	Dijon mustard	15 mL
	Salt and cayenne pepper	
2 cups	shredded Cheddar cheese (about 8 oz [250 g]), preferably aged	500 mL
2 cups	elbow macaroni	500 mL
1 tbsp	butter	15 mL
1 cup	soft bread crumbs	250 mL

1. In a large saucepan, melt butter over medium heat. Blend in flour and add bay leaf; cook, stirring, for 30 seconds. Pour in 1 cup (250 mL) of the milk, whisking constantly, until mixture comes to a boil and is very thick. Pour in rest of milk in a slow stream, whisking constantly, until sauce comes to a full boil and is smooth. Whisk in mustard.

2. Reduce heat to low; stir in cheese until melted. Remove bay leaf; season with salt and a dash of cayenne pepper to taste. Remove from heat.

3. Meanwhile, in a large pot of boiling salted water, cook macaroni for 8 minutes or until just tender. (Do not overcook; pasta continues to cook in sauce.) Drain well. Stir into cheese sauce until well coated.

4. Spoon into prepared casserole dish. In a bowl microwave remaining 1 tbsp (15 mL) butter at High for 20 seconds or until melted. Toss with bread crumbs; sprinkle over top. Bake in preheated oven for 25 minutes or untilbubbly and top is lightly browned.

Fettuccine with Mushrooms in a Creamy Tomato Sauce

12 oz	fettuccine	375 g
3 tbsp	butter	45 mL
1 lb	mushrooms (preferably wild), sliced	500 g
2 tbsp	crushed garlic	25 mL
1 1/4 cups	whipping (35%) cream	300 mL
1/2 cup	diced tomatoes	125 mL
2 tsp	freshly squeezed lemon juice	10 mL
1/3 cup	grated Parmesan cheese	75 mL
	Salt and pepper to taste	

1. In a large pot of boiling salted water, cook fettuccine 8 to 10 minutes or until *al dente*. Meanwhile, prepare the sauce.

2. In a large saucepan, melt butter over high heat. Add mushrooms and garlic; cook, stirring, 3 minutes. Stir in cream and cook about 3 minutes. Reduce heat to medium; stir in tomatoes and lemon juice. Add drained pasta and Parmesan; toss. Season to taste with salt and pepper. Serve immediately.

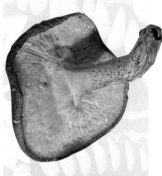

Fettuccine Alfredo

1 cup	whipping (35%) cream	250 mL
1 cup	light (15%) cream	250 mL
1/4 cup	butter, softened	50 mL
1 1/2 cups	freshly grated Parmesan cheese	375 mL
1/4 tsp	freshly ground pepper	1 mL
	Salt and nutmeg	
1 lb	fettuccine	500 g
1/4 cup	finely chopped fresh chives *or* basil or parsley	50 mL

Makes about 7 cups (1.75 L)

Here's an indispensable sauce I always have handy in the freezer to use as a base for my family's favorite pasta dishes. It's a versatile sauce and I've included several ways to serve it.

1. In a large saucepan, bring whipping cream and light cream to a boil over medium heat; boil until reduced to about 1 1/2 cups (375 mL). Reduce heat to low; whisk in butter and cheese until sauce is smooth. Add pepper; season with salt and nutmeg to taste. Keep warm.

2. Meanwhile, in a large pot of boiling salted water, cook the pasta until tender but still firm. Drain well; return to pot; pour cream sauce over. Sprinkle with herbs; toss well. Serve immediately on warm plates.

Big-Batch Tomato Sauce

2 tbsp	olive oil	25 mL
1	medium onion, finely chopped	1
2	medium carrots, peeled and finely chopped	2
1	stalk celery, including leaves, finely chopped	1
4	cloves garlic, finely chopped	4
1 tbsp	dried basil	15 mL
1 1/2 tsp	dried oregano	7 mL
1 tsp	salt	5 mL
1 tsp	granulated sugar	5 mL
1/2 tsp	pepper	2 mL
1	bay leaf	1
2	cans (28 oz [796 mL]) plum tomatoes, chopped	2
1	can (5 1/2 oz [156 mL]) tomato paste	1
1/4 cup	finely chopped fresh parsley	50 mL

1. In a Dutch oven, heat oil over medium-high heat. Add onion, carrots, celery, garlic, basil, oregano, salt, sugar, pepper and bay leaf; cook, stirring often, for 5 minutes or until vegetables are softened.

2. Stir in tomatoes, tomato paste and 1 tomato-paste can of water. Bring to a boil; reduce heat and simmer, partially covered, for 35 to 40 minutes, stirring occasionally, until slightly thickened. Remove bay leaf; stir in parsley. Let cool; pack into containers and refrigerate or freeze.

Serves 4

FROM
THE COMFORT FOOD COOKBOOK
BY JOANNA BURKHARD

Spaghetti with Meatballs

PREHEAT OVEN TO 400° F (200° C)
RIMMED BAKING SHEET, GREASED

1/2 tbsp	vegetable oil	7 mL
Half	medium onion, finely chopped	Half
1	clove garlic, minced	1
1/2 tsp	salt	2 mL
1/4 tsp	dried thyme	1 mL
1/4 tsp	pepper	1 mL
1/4 cup	beef stock	50 mL
1 tbsp	Worcestershire sauce	15 mL
1 lb	lean ground beef	500 g
1/2 cup	soft bread crumbs	125 mL
1 tbsp	finely chopped fresh parsley	15 mL
1	egg, lightly beaten	1
3 cups	BIG-BATCH TOMATO SAUCE (see recipe, page 31)	750 mL
1/2 cup	beef stock	125 mL
12 oz	cooked spaghetti	375 g

1. In a medium nonstick skillet, heat oil over medium heat. Add onion, garlic, salt, thyme and pepper; cook, stirring often, 5 minutes or until softened. Stir in beef stock and Worcestershire sauce; let cool slightly.

2. In a bowl combine onion mixture, ground beef, bread crumbs, parsley and half the beaten egg; mix well.

3. Form beef mixture into 1 1/2-inch (4 cm) balls; arrange on rimmed baking sheet. Bake in preheated oven for 22 to 25 minutes or until nicely browned. Transfer to a paper towel-lined plate to drain.

4. In a large saucepan, combine BIG-BATCH TOMATO SAUCE, cooked meatballs and beef stock. Bring to a boil, reduce heat and simmer, covered, for 15 minutes. Toss with cooked spaghetti; sprinkle with Parmesan cheese.

Serves 6

Linguine with Pecan Oriental Sauce and Salmon

TIPS

Great to serve warm, at room temperature, or cold.

•

If to be served cold, this dish can be prepared early in the day. Toss before serving.

•

Sauce can be used as a marinade or in a stir-fry, or over another pasta dish.

MAKE AHEAD

Prepare sauce up to 2 days ahead. Stir again before using.

FROM
ROSE REISMAN'S ENLIGHTENED HOME COOKING

Sauce

5 tbsp	packed brown sugar	75 mL
1/4 cup	chopped pecans	50 mL
3 tbsp	chicken stock *or* water	45 mL
2 1/2 tbsp	soya sauce	35 mL
2 1/2 tbsp	rice wine vinegar	35 mL
2 tbsp	lemon juice	25 mL
2 tbsp	sesame oil	25 mL
2 tsp	minced garlic	10 mL
1 1/2 tsp	minced ginger root	7 mL
1 1/2 cups	chopped baby corn cobs	375 mL
1 1/2 cups	thinly sliced red or green peppers	375 mL
1/4 cup	chopped green onions (about 2 medium)	50 mL
12 oz	linguine	375 g
8 oz	salmon cut into 1/2-inch (1 cm) cubes	250 g
2 cups	broccoli florets	500 mL

1. Put brown sugar, pecans, stock, soya sauce, vinegar, lemon juice, sesame oil, garlic and ginger in food processor; process until smooth and set aside. Put corn cobs, red peppers and green onions in large serving bowl.

2. In a large pot of boiling water, cook pasta according to package directions or until tender but firm. Drain and add to vegetables in bowl.

3. Meanwhile, in nonstick skillet sprayed with vegetable spray, cook salmon over high heat for 4 minutes or until just done at center; put in serving bowl.

4. Cook broccoli in boiling water or microwave for 2 minutes or until tender-crisp; add to serving bowl. Pour sauce over and toss.

Fish & Seafood

Fettuccine with Calamari in a Spicy Mediterranean Sauce

1/4 cup	olive oil	50 mL
3	cloves garlic, crushed	3
20	black olives, pitted and chopped	20
4	anchovy fillets, chopped	4
2 tbsp	drained capers	25 mL
1	can (28 oz [796 mL]) tomatoes, with juice	1
12 oz	fettuccine or tagliatelle	375 g
1 lb	calamari (squid), cut into 1/4-inch (5 mm) rings	500 g
1 tbsp	dried basil	15 mL
1 tbsp	dried oregano	15 mL
	Hot pepper flakes to taste	
1/4 cup	grated Parmesan cheese	50 mL
	Fresh chopped parsley	

1. In a large saucepan, heat oil over medium heat. Add garlic and cook until golden. Stir in olives, anchovies and capers; cook 1 minute. Add tomatoes, stirring to break up; reduce heat to medium-low and cook 20 minutes.

2. Meanwhile, in large pot of boiling salted water, cook fettuccine 8 to 10 minutes or until al dente; drain.

3. Stir calamari, basil, oregano and hot pepper flakes into sauce; cook just until calamari done, about 3 minutes. Toss sauce with drained pasta. Serve immediately, sprinkled with Parmesan and parsley.

Serves 4

**as a main course or
8 as an appetizer**

FROM
NEW WORLD NOODLES
BY BILL JONES & STEPHEN WONG

Peppered Salmon with Steamed Egg Noodles

STEAMER, PREFERABLY BAMBOO

1 tsp	whole Szechuan peppercorns	5 mL
1 tsp	black peppercorns	5 mL
1 tbsp	oyster sauce	15 mL
2 tsp	soya sauce	10 mL
1 tsp	dark soya sauce *or* mushroom soya sauce	5 mL
2 tbsp	chicken stock *or* water	25 mL
1 tsp	cornstarch	5 mL
1 lb	Chinese style steamed noodles *or* 8 oz (250 g) dried spaghetti	500 g
2 tbsp	chicken stock	25 mL
2 tsp	sesame oil	10 mL
1 cup	bean sprouts	250 mL
2	green onions, green part only, sliced diagonally	2
2 tbsp	vegetable oil	25 mL
12 oz	boneless salmon fillet, cut into 1/2-inch (1 cm) square pieces	375 g
1	clove garlic, minced	1
2	shallots, thinly sliced	2
1 tbsp	dry sherry	15 mL
	Juice of half lemon (optional)	

1. In a dry frying pan, toast Szechuan and black peppercorns over medium heat until fragrant. Coarsely grind in a pepper grinder or mortar and pestle, or by crushing with a wine bottle between two sheets of wax paper. Set aside.

2. In a small bowl, combine oyster sauce, soya sauces, stock and cornstarch; mix well. Set aside.

3. In a bowl, cover noodles with hot water and separate strands by pulling them apart with your hands. (If using pasta, prepare according to package instructions.) Drain. In a heatproof bowl, combine noodles with stock, sesame oil, bean sprouts and green onions. Mix well. Place noodle mixture in a dish or shallow bowl and

place in a steamer. Steam over medium heat for 4 minutes, or cover and microwave for 4 minutes. Keep warm.

4. In a nonstick wok or skillet, heat oil over medium-high heat for 30 seconds. Add salmon and sauté until golden, about 45 seconds on each side. Add peppercorns, garlic and shallots. Mix and cook for 30 seconds. Splash with sherry and toss for 15 seconds. Add sauce, stir gently and cook until sauce is thickened and salmon is well-coated, about 1 minute. Spoon salmon onto warm noodles. Add lemon juice and serve immediately.

Linguine with Shrimp, Red Peppers and Pine Nuts

8 oz	linguine	250 g
8 oz	shrimp, shelled, deveined and cut into pieces	250 g
2 tsp	vegetable oil	10 mL
2 tsp	crushed garlic	10 mL
2 cups	chopped red bell peppers	500 mL
1/3 cup	chopped green onions	75 mL
1/2 cup	chopped fresh basil (or 2 tsp [10 mL] dried)	125 mL
1 1/2 tsp	dried oregano	7 mL
1 1/4 cups	cold fish or chicken stock	300 mL
3 1/2 tsp	all-purpose flour	17 mL
3 1/2 oz	feta cheese, crumbled	90 g
2 tbsp	toasted pine nuts	25 mL

1. Cook pasta in boiling water according to package instructions or until firm to the bite. Drain and place in serving bowl.

2. In medium nonstick skillet sprayed with vegetable spray, sauté shrimp just until pink and just cooked, approximately 3 minutes. Drain and add to pasta.

3. In large nonstick skillet, heat oil; sauté garlic and red peppers for 3 minutes. Add onions, basil and oregano; sauté for 3 minutes.

4. Meanwhile, in small bowl, combine stock and flour until smooth. Add to red pepper mixture; simmer, stirring constantly until thickened, approximately 3 minutes. Add cheese and allow to melt. Pour over pasta. Add pine nuts, and toss.

Pasta with Salmon in Teriyaki Sauce

12 oz	long fusilli or rotini	375 g
12 oz	salmon, cut into 1-inch (2.5 cm) cubes	375 g
1 1/2 cups	thinly sliced sweet yellow or red peppers	375 mL
1 1/2 cups	chopped snow peas	375 mL

Teriyaki Sauce

1/3 cup	sherry *or* rice wine vinegar	75 mL
1/4 cup	brown sugar	60 mL
1/3 cup	water	75 mL
1/4 cup	soya sauce	60 mL
1/4 cup	vegetable oil	60 mL
2 1/2 tsp	minced ginger root	12 mL
2 1/2 tsp	crushed garlic	12 mL
1 tbsp	all-purpose flour	15 mL
2 tsp	sesame seeds	10 mL
	Parsley	

1. Cook pasta in boiling water according to package instructions or until firm to the bite. Drain and place in serving bowl.

2. In medium nonstick skillet sprayed with vegetable spray, sauté salmon until no longer pink, approximately 4 minutes. Do not overcook. Add to pasta.

3. Blanch yellow peppers and snow peas in boiling water until tender-crisp, approximately 2 minutes. Drain, rinse with cold water and add to pasta.

4. Make the sauce: In small saucepan, combine sherry, sugar, water, soya sauce, oil, ginger, garlic, flour and sesame seeds until smooth. Simmer on medium heat until slightly thickened, approximately 4 minutes. Pour over pasta, and toss gently. Garnish with parsley.

Seafood Tomato Stew over Fusilli with Fennel

1 cup	chopped fennel	250 mL
12 oz	fusilli *or* rotini	375 g
2 tsp	vegetable oil	10 mL
2 tsp	crushed garlic	10 mL
1 cup	chopped red onions	250 mL
1 cup	chopped green peppers	250 mL
1 cup	sliced mushrooms	250 mL
2	cans (19 oz [540 mL]) crushed tomatoes	2
1/2 cup	fish stock *or* chicken stock	125 mL
1/3 cup	sliced black olives	75 mL
1 tbsp	tomato paste	15 mL
2 tsp	dried basil	10 mL
1 tsp	dried oregano	5 mL
1	bay leaf	1
Pinch	cayenne	Pinch
8 oz	fresh mussels or clams	250 g
8 oz	shrimp, peeled and deveined	250 g
8 oz	squid, cleaned and sliced	250 g

1. Cook fennel in boiling water for 8 minutes, or just until barely tender. Drain and set aside.

2. Cook pasta in boiling water according to package instructions or until firm to the bite. Drain and place in serving bowl.

3. In a large nonstick saucepan, heat oil; sauté garlic, onions, green peppers and fennel for 5 minutes. Add mushrooms and cook for 3 minutes. Add tomatoes, stock, olives, tomato paste, basil, oregano, bay leaf and cayenne. Simmer on medium-low heat for 15 minutes, stirring occasionally.

4. Add seafood. Cover and simmer for 3 minutes, or until mussels are open and seafood just cooked. Pour over pasta.

Serves 4 to 6

Fettuccine with Fresh Salmon, Dill and Leeks

4 tsp	margarine or butter	20 mL
4 tsp	all-purpose flour	20 mL
2 cups	2% milk	500 mL
1/4 cup	grated Parmesan cheese	50 mL
1/4 cup	white wine	50 mL
2 tbsp	chopped onions	25 mL
1 tsp	crushed garlic	5 mL
2	leeks, washed and sliced in thin rounds	2
12 oz	fresh salmon, boned and cubed	375 g
3 tbsp	chopped fresh dill (or 1 tsp [5 mL] dried dillweed)	45 mL
10 oz	fettuccine noodles	300 g

1. In a small saucepan, melt margarine; add flour and cook, stirring, for 30 seconds. Add milk and cook, stirring constantly, until thickened, 4 to 5 minutes. Stir in cheese until melted; set aside.

2. In a large skillet, combine wine, onion, garlic and leeks; cook over medium heat for approximately 10 minutes or until leeks are softened. Add white sauce along with salmon. Cook for 2 to 3 minutes or until salmon is almost opaque, stirring gently. Stir in dill.

3. Meanwhile, cook fettuccine according to package directions or until firm to the bite. Drain and place in serving bowl. Toss with sauce.

Serves 6

Tuna Dressing over Pasta Niçoise

Sauce

1	can (6.5 oz [184 g]) flaked tuna, water-packed, drained	1
1/2 cup	chicken stock	125 mL
2 tbsp	light mayonnaise	25 mL
2 tbsp	vegetable oil	25 mL
1 tbsp	lemon juice	15 mL

1 tbsp	drained capers	15 mL
1 1/2 tsp	minced garlic	7 mL
12 oz	rotini	375 g
1 1/2 cups	chopped tomatoes	375 mL
1 1/4 cups	chopped cucumbers	300 mL
3/4 cup	chopped red onions	175 mL
1/3 cup	sliced black olives	75 mL
1/3 cup	chopped green onions	75 mL

1. Put tuna, stock, mayonnaise, oil, lemon juice, capers and garlic in food processor; process until smooth.

2. In large pot of boiling water cook pasta according to package directions or until tender but firm; rinse under cold water and drain. Put in large serving bowl, along with tomatoes, cucumbers, onions, olives, green onions and tuna sauce; toss well. Serve at room temperature or chilled.

Creamy Seafood Lasagna with Leeks and Sweet Bell Peppers

PREHEAT OVEN TO 350° F (180° C)
13- BY 9-INCH (3 L) BAKING DISH

9	lasagna sheets	9
1 tsp	vegetable oil	5 mL
2 tsp	crushed garlic	10 mL
2/3 cup	diced sweet red or green peppers	150 mL
2/3 cup	diced leeks or red onions	150 mL
1 lb	seafood, cut into small pieces (any combination of firm white fish fillets or scallops or shrimp)	500 g

Cream Sauce

1 tbsp	margarine or butter	15 mL
3 tbsp	all-purpose flour	45 mL
1 2/3 cups	seafood or chicken stock	400 mL
1 1/2 cups	2% milk	375 mL
1/4 cup	chopped fresh dill (or 1 tbsp [15 mL] dried)	50 mL

Cheese Sauce

1 1/2 cups	ricotta cheese	375 mL
1 cup	shredded Cheddar cheese	250 mL
1/3 cup	2% milk	75 mL
1/4 cup	grated Parmesan cheese	50 mL

FROM
ROSE REISMAN BRINGS HOME
LIGHT PASTA

1. Cook pasta in boiling water according to package instructions or until firm to the bite. Drain, cover and set aside.

2. In a medium nonstick skillet, heat oil; sauté garlic, sweet peppers and leeks just until tender, approximately 5 minutes. Add seafood and sauté until fish is opaque, approximately 5 minutes. Pour off excess liquid. Set aside.

3. Make the cream sauce: In a non-stick saucepan, melt margarine. Add flour and cook for 1 minute, stirring often. Slowly add stock and milk, and simmer on medium heat until just thickened, approximately 4 minutes, stirring often. Add seafood mixture and dill; remove from heat.

4. Make the cheese sauce: In a small bowl, combine ricotta and Cheddar cheeses, milk and Parmesan cheese until mixed.

5. Assembly: Place 3 lasagna sheets in baking dish. Spread one-third cheese mixture over top, then one-third seafood sauce. Place 3 more lasagna sheets over seafood sauce, repeat with one-third cheese and seafood sauce. Repeat with remaining lasagna, cheese and seafood sauce. Cover and bake approximately 30 minutes, or until hot.

Chicken

Serves 4

A traditional version of this dish would consist of shredded beef and Chinese cabbage tossed with soya sauce. For a change of pace we've used chicken breast and spiced up the sauce with chili paste and sesame seeds.

•

Shred cabbage by cutting into thin strips, starting at the tip of the leaves. If using a green cabbage cut the head in quarters, remove core and shred.

FROM
NEW WORLD NOODLES
BY BILL JONES & STEPHEN WONG

Shanghai Noodles with Shredded Chicken, Chinese Cabbage and a Spicy Sesame Sauce

1 lb	fresh Shanghai noodles or 8 oz (250 g) dried spaghetti	500 g
1 tbsp	vegetable oil, plus oil for coating noodles	15 mL
8 oz	boneless skinless chicken breast	250 g
2 tbsp	cornstarch	25 mL
3 cups	shredded Chinese cabbage or green cabbage	750 mL
1 tsp	minced ginger root	5 mL
1 tsp	minced garlic	5 mL
2 tbsp	water	25 mL
1 tbsp	dark soya sauce	15 mL
1 tbsp	chopped cilantro	15 mL
1 tsp	chili paste (or to taste)	5 mL
1 tsp	sesame oil	5 mL
1 tbsp	toasted sesame seeds, plus extra seeds for garnish	15 mL
	Sliced green onion for garnish	

1. In a heatproof bowl or pot, cover noodles with boiling water and soak for 5 minutes. (If using pasta, prepare according to package directions.) Drain, toss with a little oil and set aside.

2. On a cutting board, cut chicken into thin slices and then cut each slice into thin strips. Dredge strips in cornstarch, shaking off excess starch. Set aside.

3. In a nonstick wok or skillet, heat oil over medium-high heat for 30 seconds. Add ginger root and cook until it starts to sizzle. Add chicken and sauté until brown, about 4 to 5 minutes. Add cabbage and garlic and stir-fry until cabbage is wilted. Add water. Cook, covered, over low heat for 2 minutes.

4. Add soya sauce, cilantro, chili paste, sesame oil and sesame seeds to the mixture; toss well. Garnish with green onions and additional sesame seeds, if desired. Serve immediately.

Serves 6

TIP

Adjust spices according to taste. For a spicier flavor, increase cayenne.

MAKE AHEAD

Prepare spice mixture at any time and keep in a closed container. Coat the chicken up to a day before and refrigerate. Prepare sauce early in day. Reheat gently.

FROM
ROSE REISMAN BRINGS HOME
LIGHT PASTA

Cajun Chicken over Fettuccine

12 oz	fettuccine	375 g
12 oz	skinless boneless chicken breast cut into 2-inch (5 cm) strips	375 g

Spice Mixture

1 tsp	cayenne	5 mL
1 3/4 tsp	onion powder	8 mL
1 1/4 tsp	garlic powder	6 mL
1 tsp	paprika	5 mL
1 tsp	dried basil	5 mL
3/4 tsp	dried oregano	4 mL
2 1/2 tbsp	unseasoned bread crumbs	35 mL

Sauce

2 tsp	vegetable oil	10 mL
1 tsp	crushed garlic	5 mL
3/4 cup	chopped onions	175 mL
3/4 cup	chopped green peppers	175 mL
4 cups	canned or fresh tomatoes, crushed	1 L
1 1/2 tsp	dried basil	7 mL
1 tsp	dried oregano	5 mL
1/4 tsp	cayenne	1 mL

1. Cook pasta in boiling water according to package instructions or until firm to the bite. Drain and place in serving bowl.

2. Prepare the spices: In a small bowl, combine cayenne, onion and garlic powders, paprika, basil, oregano and bread crumbs. Coat chicken in mixture.

3. In a medium nonstick skillet sprayed with vegetable spray, sauté chicken on medium heat until no longer pink, approximately 4 minutes. Add to pasta.

4. Make the sauce: In same skillet, heat oil; sauté garlic, onions and green peppers for 5 minutes, until tender. Add tomatoes, basil, oregano and cayenne. Simmer for 20 to 25 minutes. Pour over pasta, and toss.

Serves 6

TIP

Cooking the entire chicken breast before slicing gives a moister piece.

•

If using fresh tarragon, chop 1/3 cup (75 mL) and add just before tossing entire pasta dish. Basil can replace tarragon.

MAKE AHEAD

Prepare sauce up to a day ahead. Reheat gently, adding more stock if too thick.

FROM
ROSE REISMAN'S ENLIGHTENED HOME COOKING

Bow-Tie Pasta with Chicken Alfredo Sauce

12 oz	skinless, boneless chicken breasts	375 g
Sauce		
1 tbsp	margarine or butter	15 mL
2 tbsp	all-purpose flour	25 mL
1 cup	2% milk	250 mL
1 cup	chicken stock	250 mL
2 tsp	dried tarragon	10 mL
1/4 cup	grated Parmesan cheese	50 mL
2 tsp	vegetable oil	10 mL
2 tsp	minced garlic	10 mL
1 cup	chopped onions	250 mL
1 cup	chopped red or green peppers	250 mL
12 oz	bow-tie pasta	375 g

1. In a nonstick skillet sprayed with vegetable spray, cook whole chicken breasts over medium-high heat until browned; turn over and cook for 3 minutes more, or until just done at center. Let cool slightly and slice into thin strips. Set aside.

2. In a small saucepan, melt margarine over medium heat; add flour and cook, stirring, for 1 minute. Gradually add milk and stock, stirring constantly, just until mixture thickens slightly (approximately 5 minutes). Add tarragon and cook for 2 more minutes. Add Parmesan and remove from heat.

3. Meanwhile, in a saucepan, heat vegetable oil over medium heat; add garlic and onions and sauté for 4 minutes until browned. Add red peppers and sauté for 4 minutes or until softened. Set aside. In large pot of boiling water, cook pasta according to package directions or until tender but firm; drain. Put pasta, chicken and cooked vegetables in serving bowl. Add sauce, toss and serve.

Serves 4 to 5

Bow-Tie Pasta with Chicken and Green Olives

TIP

Use bacon if pancetta is unavailable.

•

Try duck instead of chicken — it works especially well with this spicy sauce.

— Michela's —
BOSTON

FROM
THE ROBERT ROSE BOOK OF
CLASSIC PASTA

12 oz	bow-tie pasta (farfalle)	375 g
3 oz	pancetta, diced	75 g
3 oz	spicy sausage, casings removed	75 g
2 tbsp	chopped fresh rosemary (or 1/2 tsp [2 mL] dried)	25 mL
2 tbsp	chopped fresh sage (or 1/2 tsp [2 mL] dried)	25 mL
3	cloves garlic, minced	3
15	green olives, pitted	15
Pinch	hot pepper flakes	Pinch
1 1/2 cups	chicken stock	375 mL
1 tbsp	lemon juice	15 mL
1 tbsp	cornstarch	15 mL
6 oz	cooked chicken, thinly sliced	175 g
	Salt and pepper to taste	

1. In a large pot of boiling salted water, cook bow tie pasta 8 to 10 minutes or until *al dente*. Meanwhile, prepare the sauce.

2. In a large skillet, cook pancetta and sausage meat over medium-high heat, stirring to break up, until sausage is no longer pink, about 5 minutes. Stir in rosemary, sage, garlic, olives and hot pepper flakes; cook 2 minutes, stirring. Stir in chicken stock and lemon juice; cook 5 minutes. Dissolve cornstarch in 1 tbsp (15 mL) cold water; stir into sauce and cook until thickened, about 2 minutes. Stir in chicken; cook until heated through. Season to taste with salt and pepper.

3. Toss drained pasta with sauce. Serve immediately.

Orange and Pineapple Chicken Stir-Fry over Linguine

10 oz	linguine	300 g
10 oz	skinless boneless chicken breast, thinly sliced	300 g

Sauce

3 tbsp	brown sugar	45 mL
1 cup	chicken stock	250 mL
1/3 cup	orange juice	75 mL
1 1/2 tbsp	cornstarch	20 mL
2 tbsp	soya sauce	25 mL
2 tbsp	sesame oil	25 mL
1 1/2 tsp	crushed garlic	7 mL
1 1/2 tsp	crushed ginger root	7 mL
2 tsp	vegetable oil	10 mL
1 1/2 cups	chopped asparagus	375 mL
1 cup	sliced red bell peppers	250 mL
1 cup	chopped baby corn	250 mL
3/4 cup	sliced water chestnuts	175 mL
1 cup	pineapple pieces	250 mL
3/4 cup	mandarin oranges	175 mL

1. Cook pasta in boiling water according to package instructions or until firm to the bite. Drain and place in serving bowl.

2. In a large nonstick skillet sprayed with vegetable spray, sauté chicken just until it is browned but not cooked through. Remove chicken and set aside.

3. Make the sauce: In a small bowl, combine sugar, stock, orange juice, cornstarch, soya sauce, sesame oil, garlic and ginger. Mix well. Set aside.

4. In a skillet heat oil; sauté asparagus and red peppers just until barely tender, approximately 2 minutes. Add corn, water chestnuts, pineapple pieces, sauce and chicken. Cook just until chicken is no longer pink and sauce has thickened slightly, approximately 2 minutes, stirring constantly. Add mandarin oranges. Pour over pasta and toss.

Bow-Tie Pasta with Chicken, Olives and Sausage

Serves 6

TIP

If a spicy taste is not desired, use sweet sausage and omit red pepper flakes.

•

Roasted pork or turkey can replace chicken.

MAKE AHEAD

Prepare sauce early in day. Reheat gently, adding more stock if sauce thickens.

12 oz	bow-tie pasta *or* rotini	375 g
1 tsp	vegetable oil	5 mL
1 tsp	crushed garlic	5 mL
8 oz	spicy sausage, skin removed and chopped	250 g
1/3 cup	sliced black olives	75 mL
1/8 tsp	red pepper flakes	1 mL
2 cups	cold chicken or beef stock	500 mL
2 1/2 tbsp	all-purpose flour	35 mL
1 1/2 cups	thinly sliced roasted or grilled chicken	375 mL
	Parsley	

1. Cook pasta in boiling water according to package instructions or until firm to the bite. Drain and place in serving bowl.

2. In a large nonstick skillet, heat oil; sauté garlic and sausage for 5 minutes, or until sausage is no longer pink. Add olives and red pepper flakes.

3. Meanwhile, in a small bowl, combine stock and flour until smooth. Add to sausage mixture and simmer until just slightly thickened, approximately 4 minutes, stirring constantly. Add chicken and cook for 1 minute. Pour over pasta. Sprinkle with parsley, and toss.

FROM
ROSE REISMAN BRINGS HOME
LIGHT PASTA

Malay Chicken in Spiced Broth with Rice Vermicelli

1	onion	1
6	cloves of garlic	6
2 tsp	chopped ginger root	10 mL
1 1/4 tsp	fennel seeds	6 mL
1 1/2 tsp	coriander seeds	7 mL
1 tsp	cumin seeds	5 mL
1 tsp	black peppercorns	5 mL
1	star anise	1
2	cloves	2
1	1-inch (2.5 cm) piece cinnamon stick	1
2	stalks of lemon grass	2
1	chicken, about 2 to 3 lbs (1 to 1.5 kg)	1
1	bay leaf	1
1	stalk coriander, with root	1
1 1/2 tsp	salt	7 mL
2 tbsp	finely chopped chilies, preferably bird-eye chilies	25 mL
2 tbsp	soya sauce	25 mL
4 tsp	granulated sugar	20 mL
1 lb	bean sprouts	500 g
1	package (16 oz [500 g]) rice vermicelli	1
1 1/2 tbsp	red bell pepper or red chili, seeded and cut into very fine julienne	20 mL
1	can (14 oz [400 g]) coconut milk	1
1	green onion, cut into thin rings	1
	Coriander leaves for garnish	
1 tbsp	deep-fried shallots *or* onions (optional)	15 mL

1. In a food processor or blender, purée onion, garlic and ginger. Toast coriander, fennel, cumin, peppercorns, cloves, star anise and cinnamon together in a dry pan over medium heat until fragrant; immediately remove from pan. For a spicier soup, grind together to a fine powder; for a more subtle flavor, leave whole. Bruise lemon grass by hitting it with some force with the back of a knife or cleaver up the entire length of each stalk. Place chicken in a pot and add 8 cups (2 L) water; bring to a boil. Reduce heat to simmer while skimming off scum. When no more scum comes to the surface, add onion mixture, dry spices, lemon grass, bay leaf, coriander and salt. Simmer, uncovered, 1 hour or until chicken is tender. Remove chicken and strain broth, discarding solids; keep broth warm. Pull away all meat from the chicken; shred or cut into thin slices.

2. Pinch off and discard roots from bean sprouts; if desired, blanch sprouts in boiling water 5 seconds, rinse in cold water and drain. Pound chilies to a paste and mix with soya sauce and sugar; set aside in small sauce plate.

3. In a large pot of boiling water, cook rice vermicelli 3 to 4 minutes; drain. Divide noodles among 8 large individual bowls, cover with chicken, top with bean sprouts and red pepper or chili julienne. Without shaking or agitating the can, remove top two-thirds of coconut milk (this is the thick coconut cream; the remaining thin liquid can be reserved for another use or discarded). Add coconut milk to broth and bring to a boil; ladle over noodles. Sprinkle with green onion rings and coriander leaves and, if desired, sprinkle with fried shallots or onion. Serve with chili-soya sauce.

Meat

Penne with Steak, Plum Tomatoes and Pesto

6 oz	thinly sliced beef steak	150 g

Pesto Sauce

1 1/2 cups	packed fresh basil	375 mL
3 tbsp	olive oil	45 mL
3 tbsp	Parmesan cheese	45 mL
2 tbsp	toasted pine nuts	25 mL
1 1/2 tsp	minced garlic	7 mL
3 tbsp	chicken stock *or* water	45 mL
12 oz	penne	375 g
1 tsp	vegetable oil	5 mL
1 tsp	minced garlic	5 mL
1 1/3 cups	chopped onions	325 mL
1 3/4 cups	sliced mushrooms	425 mL
2 1/4 cups	chopped fresh plum tomatoes	550 mL
1/2 cup	green peas	125 mL

1. In a nonstick skillet sprayed with vegetable spray, cook beef just until desired doneness. Drain and set aside.

2. Pesto: Put basil, olive oil, Parmesan, pine nuts and garlic in food processor; process until finely chopped. Gradually add the stock through the feed tube and process until smooth. Put pesto in serving bowl.

3. In a large pot of boiling water, cook the penne until tender but firm. Meanwhile, heat oil in a nonstick skillet over medium heat; cook garlic and onions for 4 minutes until brown. Add mushrooms and sauté for 4 minutes until tender. Add tomatoes and peas and cook for 2 minutes more to heat through.

4. Place drained pasta in serving bowl along with vegetables and steak; toss and serve.

Linguine with Spicy Italian Sausage in a Red Wine Tomato Sauce

12 oz	linguine	375 g
Sauce		
2 tsp	vegetable oil	10 mL
1 tsp	crushed garlic	5 mL
1 cup	diced onions	250 mL
8 oz	spicy sausages, skinned and chopped	250 g
1/2 cup	dry red wine	125 mL
2 cups	prepared tomato sauce or BIG-BATCH TOMATO SAUCE (see recipe, page 31)	500 mL
3 tbsp	grated Parmesan cheese	45 mL

1. Cook pasta in boiling water according to package instructions or until firm to the bite. Drain and place in serving bowl.

2. Make the sauce: In a large nonstick skillet, heat oil; sauté garlic and onions just until soft. Add sausages and sauté until meat loses its pinkness, about 5 minutes.

3. Add wine and tomato sauce to sausage mixture; simmer over low heat for 15 minutes, just until sauce thickens, stirring occasionally. Pour over pasta. Sprinkle with cheese, and toss.

Creamy Baked Beefaroni

PREHEAT OVEN TO 450° F (230° C)
9- BY 13-INCH (3 L) BAKING DISH SPRAYED WITH VEGETABLE SPRAY

Meat Sauce

1 tsp	vegetable oil	5 mL
2 tsp	minced garlic	10 mL
1 cup	chopped onions	250 mL
12 oz	lean ground beef	375 g
1 3/4 cups	tomato pasta sauce	425 mL
1/2 cup	beef or chicken stock	125 mL

Cheese Sauce

1 1/2 tbsp	margarine or butter	20 mL
1/4 cup	all-purpose flour	50 mL
2 cups	2% milk	500 mL
1 3/4 cups	beef or chicken stock	425 mL
1 cup	grated Cheddar cheese (3 1/2 oz [90 g])	250 mL
1 lb	penne	500 g
1/2 cup	grated mozzarella cheese	125 mL
2 tbsp	grated Parmesan cheese	25 mL

1. In a nonstick saucepan, heat oil over medium heat. Cook garlic and onions for 4 minutes or until softened. Add beef, and cook, stirring to break it up, for 4 minutes or until no longer pink. Add tomato sauce and stock; simmer, covered, for 10 minutes or until thickened. Set aside.

2. In a saucepan, melt margarine over medium-low heat. Add flour and cook, stirring, for 1 minute. Gradually add milk and stock. Cook, stirring constantly, until sauce begins to boil. Reduce heat to low and cook for 5 minutes, stirring occasionally, until slightly thickened. Stir in Cheddar cheese and remove from heat. Combine cheese sauce and meat sauce and set aside.

3. In a large pot of boiling water, cook pasta according to package directions or until tender but firm; drain. Toss pasta with sauce and pour into prepared dish. Sprinkle with mozzarella and Parmesan cheeses and bake for 10 minutes or just until bubbly on top.

FROM
NEW WORLD NOODLES
BY BILL JONES & STEPHEN WONG

Serves 4

TIP

If you can find yard-long beans (usually in Asian markets) try them in this recipe. They're very tender and require less cooking time than regular beans.

•

If you don't have hoisin sauce, try tomato ketchup, which will also add sweetness to the dish.

Rice Noodles with Beef, Green Beans and Tomatoes

Marinade

1 tbsp	soya sauce	15 mL
1 tbsp	dark soya sauce	15 mL
	or mushroom soya sauce	
1/2 tsp	sugar	2 mL
2 tbsp	dry sherry	25 mL
1/2 tsp	freshly ground black pepper	2 mL
1 tbsp	cornstarch	15 mL
12 oz	sirloin steak, cut into thin strips	375 g
4 or 5	medium tomatoes	4 or 5
8 oz	green beans, trimmed and sliced diagonally into 2-inch (5 cm) pieces	250 g
1 lb	fresh flat rice noodles *or* 8 oz (250 g) broad vermicelli (broad rice stick noodles)	500 g
2 tbsp	vegetable oil, plus oil for coating noodles	25 mL
1	small onion, sliced	1
2 tsp	minced garlic	10 mL
2 tsp	minced ginger root	10 mL
1/2 cup	chicken stock	125 mL
1 tbsp	hoisin sauce	15 mL
	Salt and pepper to taste	

1. In a small bowl, combine ingredients for marinade and mix well. Add beef and set aside to marinate for 20 minutes or overnight in refrigerator.

2. Blanch tomatoes in boiling water for 30 seconds. Over a bowl, peel, core and seed them. Chop tomatoes into 2-inch (5 cm) cubes. Strain any accumulated juices from bowl and reserve. Place tomato chunks in a sieve over bowl. Sprinkle lightly with salt and set aside to drain.

3. In a pot of boiling salted water, cook beans until tender-crisp, about 4 minutes. Drain and set aside.

4. In a colander, break up fresh rice noodles by running hot water over them and separating strands by hand. (If using dried noodles, cover with boiling water and soak for 5 minutes; drain, coat with a little oil and set aside.)

5. In a nonstick wok or skillet, heat 1 tbsp (15 mL) of the oil over high heat until just smoking. Add onion, garlic and ginger root; stir-fry until fragrant, about 30 seconds. Add beef mixture and stir-fry until meat is cooked through, about 2 minutes. Transfer to a heatproof dish and keep warm.

6. Add chicken stock and reserved tomato juice to pan and bring to a boil over medium-high heat. Add hoisin sauce and beans; stir, cover and cook for 2 minutes. Add tomatoes and stir for 1 minute. Remove vegetables with a slotted spoon, add to beef mixture and keep warm.

7. Add remaining 1 tbsp (15 mL) oil to liquid in pan. Add noodles and stir-fry until warmed through, about 2 minutes. Transfer to a serving platter. Return beef and vegetable mixture to pan, mix well and cook briefly until sauce is slightly thickened; season to taste with salt and pepper. Pour over noodles and serve immediately.

Serves 6

TIP

A different color combination of sweet peppers makes for a beautiful dinner entrée.

MAKE AHEAD

Broil peppers early in day. Skin can be removed more quickly if, after broiling, peppers are placed in a plastic or paper bag to cool for 10 minutes, then peel. Entire dish can be prepared up to 2 hours early and served at room temperature or reheated gently in microwave.

FROM
ROSE REISMAN BRINGS HOME LIGHT PASTA

Whole Sweet Bell Peppers Stuffed with Spaghettini, Tomatoes and Prosciutto

PREHEAT OVEN TO BROIL

6	medium sweet bell peppers (green, red and/or yellow)	6
12 oz	spaghettini	375 g

Sauce

2 tsp	vegetable oil	10 mL
2 tsp	crushed garlic	10 mL
3/4 cup	diced onions	175 mL
1 3/4 cups	diced tomatoes	425 mL
1 1/4 cups	cold chicken or beef stock	300 mL
1 tbsp	all-purpose flour	15 mL
1/4 cup	chopped fresh basil (or 2 tsp [10 mL] dried)	50 mL
1 tbsp	margarine or butter	15 mL
1/2 cup	chopped prosciutto or ham	125 mL
3 tbsp	grated Parmesan cheese	45 mL

1. Broil peppers in oven or grill for 15 minutes or until charred, turning often. Let cool for 5 minutes. Remove tops of peppers and save. Peel skin and de-seed, leaving whole pepper intact. This can be done under cool running water.

2. Cook pasta in boiling water according to package instructions or until firm to the bite. Drain and place in a large bowl.

3. Make the sauce: In a large nonstick skillet, heat oil; sauté garlic and onions until soft, approximately 3 minutes. Add tomatoes and cook for 1 minute.

4. Meanwhile, combine stock and flour in small bowl; add to tomato mixture and simmer just until sauce thickens slightly, approximately 3 minutes, stirring constantly. Pour over pasta; add basil, margarine, prosciutto and cheese. Mix well. Stuff peppers until full, saving remainder as a side dish. Place pepper top over pasta, to act as lid.

Serves 8

Spicy Meatball and Pasta Stew

TIP

Ground chicken, turkey
or veal can replace the
beef.

•

Chick peas can be
replaced with kidney
beans.

MAKE AHEAD

Prepare up to a day
ahead, adding more
stock if too thick. Great
for leftovers.

FROM
ROSE REISMAN'S ENLIGHTENED
HOME COOKING

Meatballs

8 oz	lean ground beef	250 g
1	egg	1
2 tbsp	ketchup *or* chili sauce	25 mL
2 tbsp	seasoned bread crumbs	25 mL
1 tsp	minced garlic	5 mL
1/2 tsp	chili powder	2 mL

Stew

2 tsp	vegetable oil	10 mL
1 tsp	minced garlic	5 mL
1 1/4 cups	chopped onions	300 mL
3/4 cup	chopped carrots	175 mL
3 1/2 cups	beef stock	875 mL
1	can (19 oz [540 mL]) tomatoes, crushed	1
3/4 cup	canned chick peas, drained	175 mL
1 tbsp	tomato paste	15 mL
2 tsp	granulated sugar	10 mL
2 tsp	chili powder	10 mL
1 tsp	dried oregano	5 mL
1 1/4 tsp	dried basil	6 mL
2/3 cup	small shell pasta	150 mL

1. In large bowl, combine ground beef, egg, ketchup, bread crumbs, garlic and chili powder; mix well. Form each 1/2 tbsp (7 mL) into a meatball and place on a baking sheet; cover and set aside.

2. In a large nonstick saucepan, heat oil over medium heat. Add garlic, onions and carrots and cook for 5 minutes or until onions are softened. Stir in stock, tomatoes, chick peas, tomato paste, sugar, chili powder, oregano and basil; bring to a boil, reduce heat to medium-low, cover and let cook for 20 minutes. Bring to a boil again and stir in pasta and meatballs; let simmer for 10 minutes or until pasta is tender but firm, and meatballs are cooked.

Vegetables

FROM
NEW WORLD NOODLES
BY BILL JONES & STEPHEN WONG

Serves 4

TIP

Satay sauce, sometimes labeled barbecue sauce, is a pantry favorite which can be used to give almost anything a lift — from meats and seafood, to vegetables.

Satay-Glazed Vegetable Skewers with Cilantro Parmesan Noodles

PREHEAT BROILER OR, IF USING, START BARBECUE

2	zucchini, cut into a total of 16 slices, each 1 inch (2.5 cm) thick	2
2	red bell peppers, cut into a total of 16 large squares	2
16	large mushrooms	16
8	bamboo skewers, soaked in water for 4 hours	8
2 tbsp	olive oil	25 mL

Basting Sauce

1 tbsp	satay sauce (Chinese barbecue sauce)	15 mL
1 tbsp	honey	15 mL
1 tbsp	hoisin sauce	15 mL
1 tbsp	soya sauce	15 mL
1 tbsp	balsamic vinegar	15 mL
1	recipe CILANTRO PARMESAN NOODLES (see below)	1

1. Thread skewers in an attractive arrangement, using 2 pieces of each vegetable for each skewer.

2. In a small bowl, combine ingredients for basting sauce and mix well.

3. Prepare CILANTRO PARMESAN NOODLES and keep warm.

4. Brush vegetable skewers with olive oil and grill or broil 1 minute on each side. Baste each side with sauce and continue cooking for another 2 minutes on each side or until vegetables are just tender. Continue to baste during cooking to ensure that the vegetables are well coated and seasoned.

5. Divide CILANTRO PARMESAN NOODLES between 4 plates. Top with cooked vegetables; serve immediately

Serves 4

as a main course or 6 to 8 as a side dish

This quick and easy noodle dish is one of our standbys. Add some grilled chicken and a big, green salad and you can have a delicious and nutritious dinner in less than 20 minutes.

Cilantro Parmesan Noodles

1 lb	fresh Shanghai noodles *or* fresh fettuccine	500 g
2 tbsp	whipping (35%) cream	25 mL
1/2 cup	freshly grated Parmesan cheese	125 mL
1/2 cup	chopped cilantro	125 mL
	Salt and pepper to taste	

1. In a large pot of boiling salted water, cook noodles until al dente, about 3 minutes. (If using pasta, prepare according to package instructions.) Drain.

2.. Immediately return noodles to pot. Over low heat, add cream and Parmesan; mix. Add cilantro and toss thoroughly to combine. Season to taste with salt and pepper. Serve immediately.

Serves 4

**as a pasta course
or
2 as a main course**

TIP

A sparely sauced pasta, it combines the basic ingredients of pesto (basil, pine nuts, garlic) with the tartness of capers on the long, thin noodles. It works beautifully as a pasta course or as the main course of a light dinner. Fresh basil is a must here.

FROM
THE NEW VEGETARIAN GOURMET
BY BYRON AYANOGLU

Spaghettini with Capers

1/2 lb	spaghettini	250 g
1/4 cup	olive oil	50 mL
3	cloves garlic, lightly crushed but not pressed	3
2	dried red chilies	2
1/2 tsp	salt	2 mL
1/4 cup	chopped fresh basil, packed down	50 mL
2 tbsp	toasted pine nuts	25 mL
2 tbsp	drained capers	25 mL
	Grated Romano	

1. In a large pot of boiling water, cook pasta according to package directions until tender but firm.

2. Meanwhile, in a deep frying pan heat olive oil over medium-high heat for 30 seconds. Add garlic and chilies. Stir occasionally, cooking until garlic and chilies have started to turn dark brown, about 3 or 4 minutes. Remove from heat; pick out garlic and chilies and discard.

3. Place pan back on heat. Add salt and basil; stir-fry for 30 seconds until basil has wilted. Remove from heat and add pine nuts and capers. Mix well and set aside.

4. Drain pasta and transfer it to the frying pan. Toss well, making sure sauce is well distributed. Serve immediately with grated cheese on the side.

Planning a party — or going to one? This meatless dish is perfect to serve company or take along to a pot luck supper. It makes a large party dish or you can divide it into smaller portions and place into two 8-inch (2 L) casserole dishes. Enjoy one now and freeze the other for another delicious meal.

TIP

Here are some general guidelines for making pasta dishes ahead and refrigerating or freezing: Make pasta sauces up to 2 days ahead and refrigerate or freeze for up to 2 months.

•

If assembling pasta dish ahead: Cook pasta and chill under cold water; drain. Toss cold pasta with cold sauce and spoon into casserole dish. It's best to assemble casserole no more than a few hours ahead to prevent pasta from absorbing too much of the sauce.

•

To freeze: Do not add the cheese topping (it goes rubbery when frozen). Cover with plastic wrap, then with foil. Freeze for up to 2 months. Let defrost in refrigerator overnight. Increase baking time by about 10 minutes.

FROM
THE COMFORT FOOD COOKBOOK
BY JOHANNA BURKHARD

Party Pasta with Mushrooms, Spinach and Tomato

PREHEAT OVEN TO 350° F (180° C)
13- BY 9-INCH (3 L) BAKING DISH, LIGHTLY GREASED

2 tbsp	butter	25 mL
1	medium onion, finely chopped	1
4	cloves garlic, minced	4
12 oz	sliced mushrooms	375 g
1 tsp	dried basil	5 mL
1 tsp	dried oregano	5 mL
1 tsp	dried marjoram	5 mL
1 tsp	salt	5 mL
1/2 tsp	crumbled dried rosemary	2 mL
1/2 tsp	pepper	2 mL
1/4 cup	all-purpose flour	50 mL
1 1/2 cups	milk	375 mL
2 cups	light (15%) cream	500 mL
1	can (28 oz [796 mL]) tomatoes, drained, juice reserved, chopped	1
2	pkgs (10 oz [300 g] each) fresh or frozen spinach, cooked, squeezed dry and chopped	2
1 lb	bow-tie pasta (farfalle)	500 g
2 cups	shredded Fontina or Provolone cheese	500 mL
1/2 cup	freshly grated Parmesan cheese	125 mL

1. In a large saucepan or Dutch oven, melt butter over medium-high heat. Add onion, garlic, mushrooms, basil, oregano, marjoram, salt, rosemary and pepper; cook, stirring often, for 5 minutes or until softened.

2. In a bowl blend flour with just enough milk to make a smooth paste; stir in remaining milk. Gradually add milk mixture and cream to mushroom mixture, stirring constantly, until sauce comes to a full boil and thickens.

3. Add tomatoes with juice and spinach; cook, stirring often, for 3 to 5 minutes, or until piping hot. Adjust seasoning with salt and pepper to taste. Let sauce cool to room temperature.

Serves 6

This recipe is based on Chinese vegetarian mushroom dishes. Traditional Chinese vegetarian fare for religious Buddhists includes no garlic or green onions or other members of the onion family, chilies, eggs or any dairy products. It can be quite bland, oily food — yet very imaginative, often featuring bean curd and wheat gluten products for protein. Many of the most famous prepara-tions are those made to resemble meat, fish and poultry, in appearance as well as taste (the former being easier to achieve than the latter). Mushrooms are used extensively in this type of cooking and certain areas of China, like Yunnan province in the southwest, are famous for their many varieties of wild mushrooms. Use the mushrooms listed here or a combination of your own making.

FROM
THE ASIAN BISTRO COOKBOOK
BY ANDREW CHASE

Chinese Braised Mixed Mushroom Noodles

18	dried black mushrooms (shiitake)	18
1 oz	dried wood-ear fungus	25 g
12 oz	white or cremini mushrooms	375 g
1/3 cup	peanut oil or vegetable oil	75 mL
2 tbsp	Chinese rice wine *or* dry sherry or sake	25 mL
1 tbsp	soya sauce	15 mL
1/4 tsp	salt	1 mL
1 cup	sliced bamboo shoots	250 mL
1/2 cup	sliced carrots	125 mL
3/4 tsp	granulated sugar	4 mL
18 oz	dried wheat noodles *or* 2 lbs (1 kg) fresh noodles	550 g
2 tbsp	chopped green onions	25 mL
1 tsp	minced ginger root	5 mL
1/4 tsp	white pepper	1 mL
1 cup	vegetable stock or chicken stock	250 mL
2 tsp	oyster sauce	10 mL
2 tsp	cornstarch dissolved in 2 tsp (10 mL) stock or water	10 mL
8 oz	oyster mushrooms, any tough stems removed	250 g
1	package enoki mushrooms, tough ends removed	1
2 tbsp	toasted pine nuts	25 mL
1/4 tsp	sesame oil	1 mL

1. Rinse black mushrooms in cold water; soak in water to cover, 15 minutes or until soft. Drain, reserving soaking liq-uid; remove and discard stems. Pour 3 cups (750 mL) boil-ing water over dried wood-ear fungus; when cool, drain, remove stems and cut into julienne. Cut white or cremini mushrooms into halves or quarters or into thick slices.

2. In a wok or large frying pan, heat 4 tsp (20 mL) of the oil over medium–high heat; cook shiitake mushrooms until golden on both sides. Stir in 1/2 cup (125 mL) of shiitake soaking liquid, 1 tbsp (15 mL) of the rice wine and soya sauce; cook until liquid evaporates. Transfer to a bowl. Heat 1 tbsp (15 mL) oil; cook white or cremini

mushrooms until golden. Stir in remaining rice wine and salt; cook until liquid evaporates. Add to shiitake mushrooms. Heat 1 tbsp (15 mL) oil; cook bamboo shoots and carrots until edges begin to brown. Stir in sugar; cook, stirring constantly, until golden. Add to shiitake and cremini mushrooms.

3. In a large pot of boiling water, cook noodles until tender; drain. Meanwhile, in a wok, heat remaining oil over medium-high heat. Add 1 tbsp (15 mL) of the green onion and the ginger; cook 10 seconds. Stir in julienned wood-ear fungus and white pepper; cook, stirring constantly, 1 minute. Stir in remaining shiitake soaking liquid up to 1/2 cup (125 mL) and stock; bring to a boil and cook until reduced by one-third. Stir in oyster mushrooms and mushroom-vegetable mixture; cook until oyster mushrooms soften. Stir in oyster sauce and cornstarch mixture; cook until thickened. Stir in remaining green onions, enoki mushrooms, pine nuts and sesame oil. Serve over cooked noodles.

Serves 4 to 6

Pasta Primavera

12 oz	linguine	375 g
1 1/2 cups	chopped broccoli	375 mL
1 1/2 cups	snow peas	375 mL
1 cup	green peas	250 mL
1 cup	sliced zucchini	250 mL
6	asparagus spears, cut in pieces	6
1 tbsp	olive oil	15 mL
1	tomato, diced	1
1/4 cup	chopped fresh parsley	50 mL
1/2 tsp	minced garlic	2 mL
2 tbsp	olive oil	25 mL
1 3/4 cups	sliced mushrooms	425 mL
1 tsp	minced garlic	5 mL
	Salt and pepper to taste	
1 cup	whipping (35%) cream, warmed	250 mL
1/2 cup	grated Parmesan cheese	125 mL
1/3 cup	chopped fresh basil (or 1 1/2 tsp [7 mL] dried)	75 mL
1/3 cup	melted butter	75 mL
1/3 cup	pine nuts	75 mL

1. In a large pot of boiling salted water, cook linguine 8 to 10 minutes or until al dente. Meanwhile, prepare the sauce.

2. In a pot of boiling water, blanch broccoli, snow peas, green peas, zucchini and asparagus 2 minutes; refresh in cold water and drain. Set aside.

3. In a skillet heat 1 tbsp (15 mL) olive oil over medium heat. Add tomato, parsley and 1/2 tsp (2 mL) minced garlic; cook until tomato is softened, about 3 minutes; set aside.

4. In a large saucepan, heat olive oil over medium-high heat. Cook mushrooms and garlic until tender. Stir in green vegetables and tomato mixture; cook until heated through. Season to taste with salt and pepper.

5. Toss drained pasta with vegetable sauce, warmed cream, Parmesan, basil, butter and pine nuts. Serve immediately.

Penne with Brie Cheese, Tomatoes and Basil

12 oz	penne	375 g
1 1/2 lb	chopped tomatoes	750 g
2 tsp	crushed garlic	10 mL
1 cup	chopped red onions	250 mL
3 oz	diced Brie cheese	75 g
1/3 cup	sliced black olives	75 mL
2/3 cup	chopped fresh basil (or 2 tsp [10 mL] dried)	150 mL
3 tbsp	olive oil	45 mL
2 tbsp	lemon juice	25 mL
1 tbsp	red wine vinegar	15 mL
	Pepper	

1. Cook pasta in boiling water according to package instructions or until firm to the bite. Rinse with cold water. Drain and place in serving bowl.

2. Add tomatoes, garlic, onions, cheese, olives, basil, oil, lemon juice, vinegar and pepper. Mix well.

**as a pasta course
or
2 as a main course**

FROM
THE NEW VEGETARIAN GOURMET
BY BYRON AYANOGLU

Fusilli with Leeks

2	tomatoes	2
3 cups	3-color fusilli	750 mL
1 tbsp	olive oil	15 mL
2 tbsp	olive oil	25 mL
1/4 tsp	salt	1 mL
1/4 tsp	black pepper	1 mL
2 cups	finely chopped leek, green and white parts alike	500 mL
Pinch	oregano	Pinch
1 tsp	chopped fresh sage (or pinch dried)	5 mL
1/2 cup	double-strength vegetable stock (1 cup [250 mL] reduced to half)	125 mL
2 tbsp	35% cream (or 3 tbsp [45 mL] 10% cream)	25 mL
	Grated Romano	

1. Blanch tomatoes in boiling water for 30 seconds. Over a bowl, peel, core and deseed them. Chop tomatoes roughly and set aside. Strain any accumulated tomato juices from bowl; add to the chopped tomatoes.

2. In a large pot of boiling salted water, cook pasta according to package directions until tender but firm. Rinse pasta and drain. Add olive oil and toss; cover and set aside.

3. Meanwhile, in a large frying pan, heat oil over high heat for 30 seconds. Add salt and pepper and stir. Add chopped leeks and stir-fry until softened, about 2 to 3 minutes. Add oregano and sage and stir-fry for 30 seconds.

4. Stir in tomatoes and juice, mashing down the tomato. Add broth and bring to a boil, continuing to mash tomatoes and stirring for 2 to 3 minutes. Reduce heat to minimum; add cream, stirring to mix evenly, and cook for 2 to 3 minutes. Toss pasta with sauce; transfer to serving bowls. Top with grated cheese and serve immediately.

Penne with Bell Peppers, Mushrooms and Cheese

Serves 6 to 8

as an appetizer

TIP

To toast pine nuts, bake in 350° F (180° C) oven about 8 minutes or until golden and fragrant.

•

Substitute spinach for the arugula.

•

Try any soft, mild cheese — such as Havarti or brick — instead of provolone.

— *Scoozi* —
CHICAGO

FROM
THE ROBERT ROSE BOOK OF
CLASSIC PASTA

PREHEAT BROILER

2	bell peppers, any color	2
2 tbsp	olive oil	25 mL
2	cloves garlic, crushed	2
1 cup	chopped mushrooms	250 mL
1/2 cup	sliced onions	125 mL
1	green onion, chopped	1
2/3 cup	chicken stock	150 mL
2 tbsp	dry white wine	25 mL
1 1/2 cups	whipping (35%) cream	375 mL
1 tsp	minced anchovies	5 mL
1 cup	grated provolone cheese	250 mL
1/2 cup	grated Parmesan cheese	125 mL
1 lb	penne	500 g
1/4 cup	butter	50 mL
1/2 cup	toasted pine nuts	125 mL
2 oz	arugula, washed and chopped	50 g

1. Broil peppers in oven for 15 minutes or until charred, turning often. Cool. Peel skins, remove stem and seeds and cut into strips; set aside.

2. In a skillet heat oil over medium-high heat. Cook garlic, mushrooms, onions and green onion until golden brown, stirring frequently. Stir in chicken stock and white wine; cook until slightly reduced, about 2 minutes. Stir in cream and anchovies; cook until slightly thickened, about 5 minutes. Stir in cheeses; blend well.

3. In a blender or food processor, purée sauce. Strain sauce over skillet and put over low heat to keep warm.

4. In large pot of boiling salted water cook penne 8 to 10 minutes or until al dente; drain.

5. Stir butter into sauce until it melts. Toss pasta with sauce, pepper strips, pine nuts and arugula. Serve immediately.

Serves 4 to 6

Pasta with Crisp Vegetables in a Creamy Sauce

TIP

Use green (spinach) linguine for a change.

•

This is a pasta primavera that works well with any combination of fresh vegetables.

•

Try asparagus, green peppers or zucchini.

MAKE AHEAD

Make sauce early in day. Reheat gently, adding more stock if too thick.

FROM
ROSE REISMAN BRINGS HOME
LIGHT PASTA

12 oz	linguine	375 g
1 1/2 cups	chopped broccoli	375 mL
1 1/2 cups	chopped snow peas	375 mL
1 cup	thinly sliced yellow or red bell peppers	250 mL
1 cup	frozen green peas	250 mL
1 2/3 cups	chopped tomatoes	400 mL
1/2 cup	chopped fresh basil (or 2 tsp [10 mL] dried)	125 mL
1/4 cup	chopped parsley	50 mL
1/3 cup	grated Parmesan cheese	75 mL

Sauce

1 tbsp	margarine or butter	15 mL
2 tbsp	all-purpose flour	25 mL
1 cup	2% milk	250 mL
1 1/4 cups	chicken or vegetable stock	300 mL
1 1/2 tsp	crushed garlic	7 mL
	Salt and pepper	

1. Cook pasta in boiling water according to package instructions or until firm to the bite. Just before the pasta is cooked, add the broccoli, snow peas, yellow peppers and green peas to the boiling water, and cook for 2 minutes. Drain and place in serving bowl. Add tomatoes, basil, parsley and cheese.

2. Meanwhile, make the sauce: In a nonstick saucepan, melt margarine; add flour and cook for 1 minute, stirring constantly. Slowly add milk, stock, garlic and salt and pepper; stir constantly until sauce slightly thickens, approximately 4 minutes. Remove from heat. Add to pasta and toss well.

Serves 4 to 6

Rotini with Tomatoes, Black Olives and Goat Cheese

TIP

Substitute rotini or medium shell pasta for the noodles.

MAKE AHEAD

Make early in day. Toss well just before serving.

FROM
ROSE REISMAN BRINGS HOME LIGHT COOKING

1 tbsp	vegetable oil	15 mL
1 1/2 tsp	crushed garlic	7 mL
1 cup	chopped onions	250 mL
1	can (19 oz [540 mL]) tomatoes, puréed	1
1/4 cup	sliced pitted black olives	50 mL
1 tsp	dried basil (or 2 tbsp [25 mL] chopped fresh)	5 mL
	Red pepper flakes	
2 oz	goat cheese	50 g
12 oz	rotini	375 g
1 tbsp	grated Parmesan cheese	15 mL
	Chopped fresh parsley	

1. In a large nonstick saucepan, heat oil; sauté garlic and onions for 5 minutes. Add tomatoes, olives, basil, and red pepper flakes to taste; cover and simmer for 10 minutes, stirring often. Add goat cheese, stirring until melted.

2. Meanwhile, cook pasta according to package directions or until firm to the bite. Drain and place in serving bowl. Toss with sauce. Sprinkle with Parmesan cheese and garnish with parsley.

Stuffed & Baked

Serves 4 to 5

Pasta Shells Stuffed with Cheese in a Creamy Tomato Sauce

TIP

Ricotta cheese is available in 5% and 10% fat — to reduce fat, use the 5% variety.

•

Always cook an additional pasta shell or two; it will give you a sample to taste for doneness, and you will have extra if any tear.

— Umberto al Porto —
VANCOUVER

FROM
THE ROBERT ROSE BOOK OF CLASSIC PASTA

PREHEAT OVEN TO 375° F (190° C)
13- BY 9-INCH (3 L) BAKING DISH

1/4 cup	whipping (35%) cream	50 mL
8 oz	jumbo pasta shells or 12 manicotti shells	250 g
1 cup	ricotta cheese	250 mL
1/2 cup	grated Parmesan cheese	125 mL
1/4 cup	finely chopped chives or green onions	50 mL
1/4 cup	shredded Havarti, brick or fontina cheese	50 mL
2	egg yolks	2
2 cups	prepared tomato sauce	500 mL
1/3 cup	grated Parmesan cheese Chopped chives	75 mL

1. Butter bottom of baking dish. Pour cream into dish.

2. In a large pot of boiling salted water, cook jumbo pasta shells 8 to 10 minutes or until tender; drain. Rinse under cold water, drain and set aside.

3. In a bowl, stir together ricotta, Parmesan, chives, Havarti and egg yolks. Stuff pasta shells and place in baking dish. Pour tomato sauce over shells; sprinkle with Parmesan. Cover dish tightly with aluminum foil.

4. Bake until heated through, about 20 minutes. Serve sprinkled with chopped chives.

Manicotti Shells Filled with Cheese and Smoked Salmon Bits

PREHEAT OVEN TO 350°F (180°C)
13- BY 9-INCH (3 L) BAKING DISH

12	manicotti shells	12
1 1/2 cups	ricotta cheese	375 mL
1	egg	1
2 1/2 oz	chopped smoked salmon	60 g
1/4 cup	finely chopped green onions	50 mL
3 tbsp	fresh chopped dill (or 1 tsp [5 mL] dried)	45 mL
2 tbsp	2% milk	25 mL
2 tbsp	grated Parmesan cheese	25 mL
1 1/2 cups	prepared tomato sauce *or* BIG-BATCH TOMATO SAUCE (see recipe, page 31)	375 mL

1. Cook pasta in boiling water according to package instructions or until firm to the bite. Drain, cover and set aside.

2. In bowl, combine ricotta cheese, egg, salmon, green onions, dill, milk and Parmesan cheese; mix until smooth. Fill pasta shells.

3. Pour half tomato sauce in bottom of large baking dish. Place pasta shells over sauce and pour other half tomato sauce over pasta. Cover and bake for 15 to 20 minutes or until hot.

Lasagna with Zucchini, Red Pepper and Mushrooms

PREHEAT OVEN TO 350° F (180° C)
13- BY 9-INCH (3 L) BAKING DISH SPRAYED WITH VEGETABLE SPRAY

9	lasagna noodles	9
1 tbsp	vegetable oil	15 mL
1 1/2 tsp	crushed garlic	7 mL
1 cup	chopped zucchini	250 mL
1 cup	chopped onion	250 mL
1 cup	diced sweet red pepper	250 mL
1 cup	sliced mushrooms	250 mL
1	can (19 oz [540 mL]) tomatoes, crushed	1
2 cups	tomato sauce	500 mL
1 tsp	dried basil	5 mL
1 tsp	dried oregano	5 mL
1 1/2 cups	2% cottage cheese	375 mL
1/2 cup	2% milk	125 mL
1/2 cup	grated Parmesan cheese	125 mL
8 oz	mozzarella cheese, shredded	250 g

1. Cook lasagna according to package directions or until firm to the bite. Drain and set aside.

2. In large nonstick skillet, heat oil; sauté garlic, zucchini, onion, red pepper and mushrooms until softened, approximately 8 minutes. Add tomatoes, tomato sauce, basil and oregano; cover and simmer for 15 minutes, stirring occasionally.

3. Meanwhile, in food processor, combine cottage cheese, milk and Parmesan cheese. Set aside.

4. To assemble, arrange 3 lasagna noodles in bottom of baking dish. Pour one-third of tomato sauce over top. Pour half of the cottage cheese mixture over top. Repeat layering once. Top with remaining 3 noodles. Pour remaining tomato sauce over top; sprinkle with mozzarella cheese. Bake, uncovered, for 30 minutes or until hot. Let stand for 15 minutes before serving.

Serves 4 to 6

Baked Orzo and Beans

TIP

Orzo — a jumbo rice lookalike — may be the most versatile of all pastas. This recipe comes from a long line of similarly baked Greek dishes, but borrows from Italian cuisine in its cheese topping. Use a plainer tomato sauce (mine may be too piquant) and omit the sautéed red onion, and you'll have a dish that delights young children, who seem to have a natural affinity to orzo (maybe because it's so much fun to pick up individual grains with tiny fingers).

FROM
THE NEW VEGETARIAN GOURMET
BY BYRON AYANOGLU

PREHEAT OVEN TO 350° F (180° C)
10-CUP (2.5 L) CASSEROLE WITH LID

2 1/2 cups	orzo	625 mL
1 tbsp	olive oil	15 mL
1/2 cup	sliced red onions	125 mL
2	tomatoes, roughly chopped	2
2 cups	prepared tomato sauce *or* BIG-BATCH TOMATO SAUCE (see recipe, page 31)	500 mL
2 cups	cooked red kidney beans	500 mL
1 cup	tomato juice	250 mL
1 cup	shaved Parmesan cheese	250 mL
1 tbsp	extra virgin olive oil	15 mL
	Few sprigs fresh parsley, chopped	
	Grated Romano (optional)	

1. In a large pot of boiling salted water, cook orzo until *al dente*, about 10 minutes.

2. Meanwhile, in a skillet, heat oil over high heat for 30 seconds. Add onions; cook, stirring, for 1 or 2 minutes, until slightly charred. Remove from heat and set aside.

3. When the orzo is cooked, drain well and transfer to casserole. Add sautéed onions to orzo and stir to combine. Add tomatoes and tomato sauce; mix thoroughly. Add cooked beans; fold until evenly distributed.

4. Cover the orzo mixture and bake, covered, for 30 minutes. Remove from oven and mix in tomato juice. Top with Parmesan shavings and return to the oven, uncovered, for another 10 to 12 minutes, until the cheese is melted. Serve on pasta plates, making sure each portion is topped with some of the melted cheese. Drizzle a few drops of extra virgin olive oil on each portion and garnish with chopped parsley. Serve immediately, with optional Romano as an accompaniment.

Lasagna with Bell Peppers, Eggplant and Zucchini

Serves 8

TIP

Always cook an additional lasagna noodle or two; it will give you a sample to taste for doneness, and you will have extra if any tear.

•

Lasagna cuts into portions more easily if you let it stand 10 minutes before serving.

— *Locanda Veneta* — *LOS ANGELES*

FROM
THE ROBERT ROSE BOOK OF CLASSIC PASTA

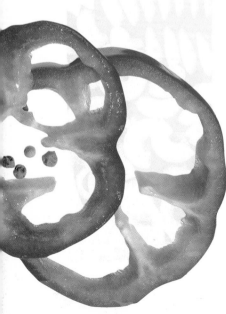

PREHEAT BROILER
13- BY 9-INCH (3 L) BAKING DISH

9	lasagna noodles	9
2	red or yellow peppers	2
1/3 cup	olive oil	75 mL
1	zucchini, halved lengthwise and thinly sliced	1
1	small eggplant, halved lengthwise and thinly sliced	1
	Flour for dusting vegetables	
2 tbsp	olive oil	25 mL
8 oz	mushrooms, sliced	250 g
1/4 cup	chopped onions	50 mL
3 cups	prepared tomato sauce	750 mL
12 oz	mozzarella cheese, sliced	375 g
1/2 cup	grated Parmesan cheese	125 mL

1. In a large pot of boiling salted water, cook lasagna noodles 6 to 8 minutes or until tender; drain. Rinse under cold water, drain and set aside.

2. Broil peppers in oven, turning often, for 15 minutes or until charred. Cool. Peel skins, remove stem and seeds, and cut into strips; set aside.

3. In a large skillet, heat 1/3 cup (75 mL) olive oil over medium-high heat. Dust zucchini and eggplant slices with flour. Keeping zucchini and eggplant separate, cook vegetables in batches until barely cooked; remove from pan and set aside. Add 2 tbsp (25 mL) olive oil to pan; cook mushrooms and onions until soft and set aside.

4. Preheat oven to 350° F (180° C). Spread 3/4 cup (175 mL) of the tomato sauce in bottom of baking dish. Arrange 3 noodles in dish. Layer with all the eggplant, half of the pepper strips, half of the mozzarella, half of the Parmesan and 1 cup (250 mL) of the tomato sauce. Arrange 3 noodles over top. Layer with zucchini, mushroom mixture, remaining pepper strips and remaining mozzarella. Top with remaining noodles, tomato sauce and Parmesan cheese. Cover dish tightly with aluminum foil.

5. Bake until hot, about 45 minutes.

Index

GREAT COOKBOOKS FROM ROBERT ROSE

Here are the bestselling full-sized cookbooks from which we've selected the recipes in this book.

Byron Ayanoglu's *The New Vegetarian Gourmet* creates fast and easy culinary magic. These exquisite vegetarian recipes are a must for people who love great tasting food but want all the benefits of vegetarian meals.
ISBN 1-896503-26-8

Johanna Burkhard's *Comfort Food Cookbook* brings you over 100 fast, easy recipes for the most comforting dishes you've ever tasted. So relax. This is the kind of old-fashioned food that just makes you feel good.
ISBN 1-896503-07-1

In *New World Noodles,* Bill Jones and Stephen Wong have created the next step in pasta books. Here's a fresh approach to mealtime, blending Eastern and Western flavors to give you a wide range of tantalizng dishes.
ISBN 1-896503-01-2

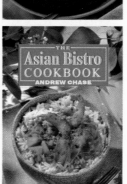

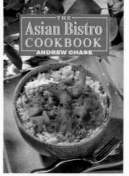

With *The Asian Bistro Cookbook,* Andrew Chase brings you the best of China, Japan and Thailand — plus tanatalizing dishes from the Philippines, Korea, Vietnam, Indonesia and Taiwan. They're unusual and delicious.
ISBN 1-896503-21-7

Here's the book that established author Rose Reisman as a major force in the world of cookbook publishing. Now with more than 200,000 copies sold, *Light Cooking* proves that healthy eating doesn't have to be dull.
ISBN 1-896503-00-4

Everyone loves pasta. And here bestselling author Rose Reisman has created over 175 deliciously light pasta recipes. You won't believe how these pasta dishes can be so low in fat and calories — yet so full of flavor.
ISBN 1-896503-02-0

Everyone wants to provide their families with healthy, delicious meals. But these days, who has the time? You do! And Rose Reisman proves it in this collection of 175 light and easy recipes — all low in fat but full of taste.
ISBN 1-896503-12-8

Here's the ultimate book for pasta lovers, with over 100 recipes specially selected from the menus of top North American restaurants and adapted for home cooking. They're as simple to make as they are delicious.
ISBN 1-896503-03-9

AVAILABLE AT BOOKSTORES AND OTHER FINE RETAILERS